Sunset

Barbecue
Building Book

By the Editors of Sunset Books and Sunset Magazine

LANE PUBLISHING CO.
MENLO PARK, CALIFORNIA

Design Credits

F. J. AGARDY: page 25 (bottom left)

ARMSTRONG AND SHARFMAN, Landscape Architects: page 30 (top)

ROBERT BABCOCK AND ASSOC., Landscape Architects: page 23 (right)

ROBERT BIER: page 36 (left)

BENSON CALIFORNIA BARBECUES: page 37 (right)

CHAR-BROIL: 11, 13 (right)

CHARMGLOW: page 21 (top)

CHESTER CARJOLA, Architect: page 33 (right)

NED DOLL: page 25 (bottom right)

ERIKSSON AND PETERS, Landscape Architects, page 25 (top)

DENNIS FISCHER: page 19 (bottom)

JOHN D. GRAY: page 12 (left)

KEN HAYASHI, Landcape Architect: page 30 (bottom)

EARLE G. HEDEMARK: page 61 (left)

R. C. HORNE: page 42

JENN-AIR CORPORATION: pages 35 (top right), 53

HERBERT KAMEON, Architect: page 24 (top)

FRED KNIPE: page 15 (bottom left)

JOHN C. LEISSRING: pages 38-39

MARKS, SCHOFIELD AND GOBELS, Architects: page 35 (top left)

JOSEPH MOREY: pages 14-15 (top)

CHANDLER MURPHY: pages 28-29 (top)

BYRON L. NISHKIAN: page 22 (left)

NORWOOD AND DE LONGE: pages 34 (bottom), 35 (bottom)

VLADIMIR OSSIPOFF, Architect: pages 22-23, 27 (right), 28 (left, bottom right)

LEON PETERS: page 31 (top)

RUSHMORE AND WOODMAN, Architects: pages 36-37 (top)

SPLENDA & YAMAMOTO, Landscape Architects: page 14 (top)

DR. ROGER STARK: page 40

MORGAN STEDMAN, Architect: page 32 (left)

STEDMAN AND WILLIAMS, Architects: pages 32-33

TENNESSEE VALLEY AUTHORITY: page 14 (bottom)

THE FRANCISCAN FORGE AND INTERIORS: page 31 (bottom)

WARREN THOMPSON, Architect: page 18 (top)

A. K. TOBIN: page 41 (bottom)

WILLIAM TURNER: page 26 (left)

VALLEY ROCKERY: page 65

HENRY VAN SIEGMAN, Landscape Architect: pages 12-13

RICHARD G. WATHEN: page 34 (top)

Artwork: Most of the illustrations for this book are the work of Joe Seney, with the exception that the plan sketches (pages 68-79) were primarily by E. D. Bills.

Cover: Photographed by Ernest Braun at the home of Glen O. Smallcomb, Atherton, California. Metal barbecue fixture custom made by Benson California Barbecues, Sunnyvale, California.

Sunset Books
  Editor, David E. Clark
  Managing Editor, Elizabeth L. Hogan

Eighteenth printing November 1987

Contents

Special Features

Planning Your Barbecue

When you sit down to pick out a type of barbecue that just fits your family, your final selection will be influenced by several factors. Your family's daily way of living, the friendliness of your climate, the practical functions that you expect a barbecue to perform, and the cost you feel you can afford.

Permanent or portable?

Your first decision involves the choice between a portable or fixed installation. Each type has its advantages.

One of the many excellent portables now on the market may be all you need. A portable would surely catch your favor if you prefer not to confine your barbecuing to one spot in your garden, if you don't want to rearrange your backyard to take in a permanent structure, or if your climate is so unpredictable that you must have a barbecue that can be drawn under shelter from time to time.

On the other hand, you may conclude that flexibility in a barbecue is no real advantage to you, because you have only one suitable location, and you might as well build a permanent installation there.

Outdoors or in?

If you wish to enjoy charcoal-broiled meat the year around, or if your climate is so disagreeable that you prefer not to cook outdoors, you should probably give consideration to an indoor barbecue.

If your choice favors this type, however, you'd better check over your ideas with a contractor, architect, or building inspector. Construction of an indoor unit involves technical problems in design and a few puzzles in ventilation control which are best discussed with a professional (see page 36).

Cooking needs

The next consideration is the cooking capacity that you will require. Remember that your family will probably be eating ten meals from your barbecue to every one that it shares with guests, so plan first to satisfy the family's everyday appetites.

You'll need a grill, of course, so the problem narrows down to a review of the cooking devices that may replace or supplement it. For what meals will you be using the barbecue? If for breakfasts, will you require a hot plate for frying bacon, eggs, or hot cakes? For dinners, will you be serving in generous quantity and thus require a spit for cooking roasts and fowl? Do you intend to oven-bake casserole and pastry dishes outdoors, or will you prepare these in the kitchen? Perhaps someone in your family has cultivated a taste for shish kebab or for meat roasted in a Chinese oven.

How much added capacity will you require for company dinners? If your family's needs are satisfied by a simple grill installation, but if you like to entertain, you may want to add a spit assembly to provide for holiday crowds. For really large gatherings, say two or three hundred guests, you should consider a pit-barbecue.

There's one important cooking feature that people often overlook—enough working space beside the grill on which to set plates, pots, kettles, and other provisions. This may be built-in or it may be provided by collapsible tables.

Non-cooking needs

Plan to make your barbecue work for you during the rest periods between barbecue meals. The average barbecue spends only a small portion of its life serving up meals, and for most of the time, it stands idle. You may consider this a challenging waste of potential storage and working space.

For instance, a large counter top can serve as a shelf for parking clothes baskets if located near the drying yard. Or it might double as a garden work bench. With a small sink fitted into it, it can be used for cleaning and soaking pots and other garden implements.

The storage cabinets beneath can be filled with more than barbecue gear. You can store gardening equipment in them. There might even be room for a soil bin. If the unit is near the play yard, its cabinets could be used to conceal toys and rubber playthings from the puppy or to protect them from rain. The space may also be used for stacking firewood for the indoor fireplace, or for storing lounge cushions through the winter.

Cost factors

The type of unit you select should be one that has the endorsement of your checkbook. You can spend almost any amount that you choose.

There is no point in scrimping on the quality of materials, equipment, and workmanship. You are buying long-term enjoyment, and therefore should select materials and fixtures that will not rust out or break down under the extremes of temperature to which a barbecue unit is subjected.

You can control costs by following a few sensible practices. One is to stay within standard dimensions, so you can buy ready-made fixtures instead of having them hand-tailored. Another is to build your installation piecemeal. Work out your complete plan first, then put the unit together a little at a time. Conceivably, you might take three summers to complete a barbecue-fireplace-oven-storage combination. You can also acquire the fixtures in a similar manner—starting

off with a simple grill, later adding the elevating assembly, and later still a rotating spit.

Appearance

It's hard to set up any rules as to style and appearance. If your home is simple and rustic, choose a simple barbecue design. If your house and garden are formal, a carefully designed architectural composition is in order. Just keep the barbecue style consistent with the rest of the house. Beware of a

STYLE SHOULD HARMONIZE with house and garden.

design that will dominate your garden—a tall unit may look at home among trees, but gaunt and ill at ease among low plantings. Select materials that harmonize with those already embedded in existing garden masonry, your house, or other buildings on your lot.

Locating your barbecue

When you have agreed upon the type of barbecue that fits your family's needs, the next big problem is selecting a location for it.

Of course, if you have decided upon a portable, there is no problem, for you will be able to set it up wherever your fancy favors. And if you plan on an indoor installation, only a few factors have to be considered, for your choice of locations is pretty well limited to kitchen, pantry, dining room, and recreation room. But if your preference is for an outdoor unit that will have to be fitted into an existing garden, you will have some figuring to do.

The first step is to look over your garden—and pick out the most livable spot in it. Wherever your family likes to gather, that's the place to put your barbecue. It might be a spread of back lawn, a terrace or patio, an indoor-outdoor room, a garden house, or a sheltered porch. If you have a swimming pool, you will probably want the barbecue in close proximity.

Perhaps your yard doesn't contain a clear area that is used for outdoor living, and you may have to start from scratch. If you do, remember that adding a barbecue area can create an entire outdoor room. Rather than have such a room grow in odd bits and pieces, why not plan it through in the beginning? Make a thorough job of it, even if it leads you into building an entire terrace alongside the living room, extending an existing porch or walling-in a patio.

It may be that you can use the installation to redeem some section of the garden which is not very attractive—say, a corner that blackberry vines took over, a dusty vegetable patch the children abandoned, or a bleak side wall of the garage. Maybe you can convert your service yard or even the driveway into an outdoor room. And if you have a hillside lot, it may be in need of a retaining wall—an excellent structure to combine with a barbecue.

Wherever you put it, allow enough level area for dining and for working around the barbecue.

Sheltered from the weather?

Your barbecue area should have positive protection from wind and sun. As a matter of fact, there are few localities where a barbecue can be enjoyed for many months of the year without some form of weather control. Sometimes, a barbecue unit will be built in the open air, and after a few months it will begin to gather windscreens around itself, then a permanent wall or two, followed by an openwork roof which later closes over, until, finally, the barbecue vanishes inside a completely enclosed shelter.

Your site should take full advantage of existing protections, such as the side of the house, wall of the garage or potting shed, or a corner where a wing meets the main house. Planted windscreens or existing fences will help if they cut across the path of the prevailing winds and if they provide relief from the late slanting rays of the sun. Trees furnish fine natural shelter, although low-hanging

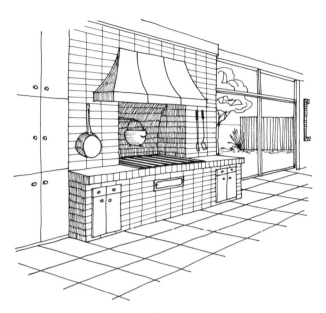

INDOOR BARBECUE offers all-weather enjoyment.

branches can be damaged by the smoke and heat from an open fire. Charcoal grills, however, do them no harm.

If your backyard climate is gentle enough so you don't have to wall-in your barbecue, face the unit into the prevailing breeze or sideways to it to insure good draft. Some builders recommend side exposure because it prevents too strong a draft.

Accessible to the kitchen?

It is well to remember that a good part of a barbecue meal is prepared in the kitchen, brought out to the barbecue, and the "remains" returned to the kitchen afterward. Ideally, this shuttle-service should be routed over level paths, to avoid carrying loaded trays across uncertain ground.

Approved by the authorities?

If the barbecue site borders your fence line or extends to an outside corner, you may have to check with your local building inspector to make certain that you won't be violating any rules about setback. Some municipalities require a building permit.

Most localities are very strict about what may or may not be done with outdoor fires. If your plan calls for a fireplace, you will have particular need to check the barbecue and its location with your local fire marshal.

How about utilities?

Utility connections are not absolutely essential, but they can add to the convenience and pleasure of cooking and eating outdoors.

Electric outlets eliminate snaggles of extension cord, and they provide a means for operating motor-driven spits and skewers, or connecting electric appliances. Electric lights have obvious advantages, too.

All the water you need for cooking and fire control may be obtainable from a nearby hose bib, but if you plan for a sink installation, you will have to cut into the water line and run a pipe to the barbecue. While you're about it, you may want to bring out a pipe from the hot-water heater for dish washing. A sink also requires drain connections, either into a sewer or a gravel drainage bed.

Hot plate and oven installations often require gas. Some outdoor units burn gas, and others have charcoal igniting jets.

How far will you have to go from your chosen site to tap into the particular utility lines that you may want to use? A long trench dug from the house to a distant point in the yard is sure to disturb some of your plantings. Of course, you may be able to bring in electricity by overhead wire rather than buried conduit, and, possibly, your water or gas pipes may be disguised as exposed pipe railings. LP gas (liquefied petroleum, available in bottled form) is a simple and effective way to solve your gas needs with a minimum of fuss and bother.

Build it yourself or have it built?

Sooner or later you will approach the question of whether to build a barbecue yourself or to have someone else put it together for you. There are advantages to both methods.

Almost any outdoor barbecue can be constructed in a few week-ends by an amateur with a moderately skilled hand and a feeling for materials. The completed structure may not look as well built as a contractor's job and it probably won't materialize as rapidly in the garden, but it is generally a very satisfying and worthwhile accomplishment.

If a contractor builds the barbecue for you, the job will naturally cost more than if you built it yourself. But there may be sound reasons for making the extra investment: A contractor will usually guarantee the job and assure you of lasting satisfaction with the unit; your garden will be trampled under for a shorter period than if you did the work; someone else takes over the chore of estimating, ordering, and assembling materials; and you can save your back muscles for another spring.

In general, if you want an indoor grill, a barbecue-fireplace combination, or one that needs a fortress-like foundation, you are better off dealing with a reliable contractor than attempting it yourself. Drop-in grills and smaller units are a different story. Some masonry contractors won't bother with a simple outdoor grill. At any rate, labor costs on a small installation are much higher in proportion than on a large one.

If you decide to deal with a contractor, first select a plan from this book or draw one of your own and work out rough specifications, then ask two or three masonry contractors or brickmasons to estimate the job (find them in the classified telephone directory under Contractors-Masonry). They will need to know what materials are to be used, principal dimensions, equipment to be installed and by whom it will be furnished, whether the site you have staked out is on the level or at the top of a lot of steps, and what type of soil will be encountered.

If you decide to do the work yourself, you will find it helpful to approach the project in a systematic fashion. Here are some suggested steps:

- Read the chapters in this book that deal with barbecue construction specifications and the use of materials.

- Secure catalogues and price lists from barbecue equipment dealers (see pages 44-49).

- Select a plan from this book or draft one of your own to scale on squared paper. Make certain that the equipment you intend to buy will fit it.

- Check with the building inspector or fire marshal to determine if there are any local regulations that you will have to follow.

- Estimate the materials required and make a list of tools and equipment you will have to buy, borrow, or rent.

- Figure how you are going to transport heavy materials to the site. By wheelbarrow? Improvised rigging? Chute? Work out a schedule for delivering the materials and equipment.

Types of Barbecues

The next time you are on your way over to a neighbor's to inspect his new barbecue you could have any one of a hundred different images of barbecues running through your mind. His barbecue could be anything from a hole in the ground to a beautiful masonry installation almost large enough to live in. He may even show you a unit that is built into his kitchen counter and burns gas instead of charcoal. Or, the new acquisition may be a simple portable unit.

If you turn to the dictionary for help, you will learn that the word comes from "barbacoa," a West Indian word for rack or frame, and that a "barbecue is an occasion for roasting a whole carcass, as an ox or a hog."

A hundred years ago, when whole oxen were conveniently roaming the foothills, it was the custom to roast meat in large chunks. A carcass was usually cooked in what we know as a pit barbecue. The meat was either buried in a deep trench filled with live coals and hot stones, or it was supported above a bed of fire contained in a shallow rock-lined pit.

The old-time pit was simply a device for cooking food by exposing it directly to heat radiating from live coals. Essentially, that's exactly what the present-day barbecue is.

Almost every type of barbecue has two main things in common with other types: a shelf, or *grill*, to hold the food; and below that another shelf, or *grate*, to hold the fire.

Both are supported by the walls of a *firebox*, which also serves to contain the heat of the coals.

Open space below the firebox may be occupied by an *ash pit*, if the grate is slotted to let ashes drift down, or by a storage cabinet or warming oven, if the grate is a solid plate.

Doors or openings in the barbecue wall provide draft to the coals or access to the compartments used for fire, ashes, or storage. In the way of accessories, the barbecue may have a fixture for raising or lowering either the grill or the grate, a revolving *spit* supported above the grill for roasting heavy cylindrical cuts of meat, a set of *skewers* rested across the grill opening for cooking small cubes of meat, or a *hot plate* to use in place of the grill for griddle cooking.

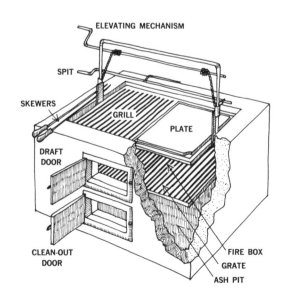

Firepit-barbecue

Where local fire ordinances permit its use, an open firepit makes the simplest type of barbecue. It consists of a shallow saucer dug into the garden soil or the patio surface, which is lined with a fire-re-

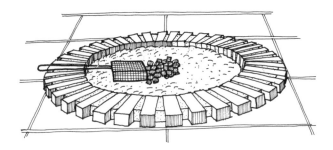

sistant material such as rocks or bricks, and fitted with a grill or grate.

The firepit is not to be confused with the deep-trench pit-barbecue. Rarely found in a permanent installation of steel or stone, this old-timer is usually dug on the spot to feed large gatherings of people.

Low-level grill

The low-level masonry barbecue is a simple enclosure of brick or stone, capped with a grill. Its low height makes it unobtrusive and easy to blend into an informal or natural garden. When made

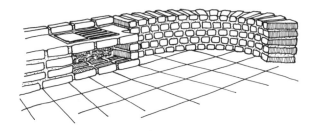

of brick, it is often built into the seat wall or a low retaining wall. Those built of stone provide a pleasing rustic feature, one step removed from a campfire, at home in a primitive garden setting.

Counter-height grill

The basic unit of the barbecue line is the counter-height grill. This unit is usually quite popular with the chef, because of its comfortable working height, and the fact that it's usually paired-off with

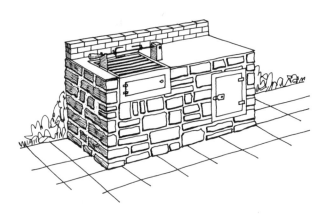

a good deal of counter space. It is also adaptable to many variations in design. Through minor changes, it can accommodate any type of grill or grate, stationary or elevating; it can be built with open space below for a warming oven, storage cabinet, or a fuel locker; or indoors it may be used as a fireplace. It can also be built with or without metal doors or draft openings.

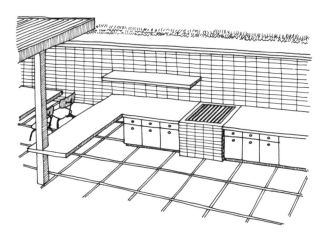

The counter-height grill frequently turns up indoors, where it may be installed in the kitchen counter, constructed free-standing under a ventilating hood, or built into a raised fireplace.

When a counter-height barbecue is made with a hot plate that seals the top of the firebox, it should have a short chimney to carry off smoke.

There have been many innovations in indoor barbecues; see pages 32-37.

Barbecue-fireplace

The combination of barbecue and outdoor fireplace furnishes both food and warmth although, once again, fire ordinances should be checked with the local fire marshal before constructing an outdoor fireplace. There are two main ways of blending these units.

The outdoor fireplace may be built with provisions within its firebox to support a grill and with brackets on its facing to hold a revolving spit or shish kebab attachment. This makes a compact combination, but unless it is carefully designed, it is likely to force you to choose between food and heat, as it may be inconvenient to use for cooking while a fire is blazing on the hearth.

The other combination involves the pairing of a counter-height barbecue with a separate fireplace. This serviceable blend provides social fire

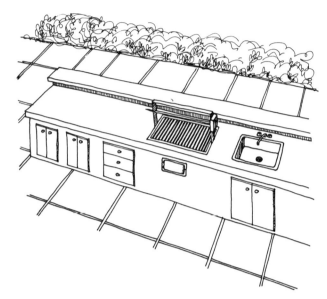

SINK AND CABINETS *are among the many extras that can be installed for outdoor cooking enjoyment.*

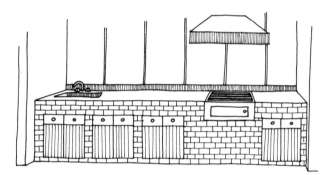

COUNTER SPACE *paired with barbecue is handiest.*

and cooking coals simultaneously. It can also be planned with generous counter areas by adding other counter-height units to balance the visual appeal of the barbecue.

Kitchen extras

There are many extras that expand an outdoor barbecue installation into an outdoor kitchen. These units supplement the barbecue by providing facilities for complete meal preparation and clean-up, enlarging the counter surface available for preparing and serving meals, and by reducing the shuttle service between the kitchen and the outdoor barbecue.

Storage cabinets. Simple masonry cabinets, with or without doors, provide space for storing fuel, barbecue equipment, utensils, and tools. With the addition of insulation and waterproofing, a cabinet can be turned into an icebox; with some plumbing and a sink, storage cabinets can become areas for

dishwashing and meal preparation. On a fancier level, these compartments can be used for a bar or as a housing for an electric refrigerator, dishwasher, or garbage-disposal unit.

Types of ovens. There are four kinds of ovens popularly called upon to assist the barbecue. The most common are the warming ovens, installed either below or alongside the firebox. They are handy for warming rolls, garlic bread, and plates, and for storing barbecue gear between meals.

A second type of oven is the baking oven with a firebox of its own, vented through a chimney that often belongs to an outdoor fireplace. Once it is fired up, it can do almost anything an indoor oven can do.

The third variety is known variously as a Spanish, Italian, Mexican, or Dutch oven. Whatever the nationality, the operating principles are the same. The fire is built on the oven floor, allowed to burn for several hours, then raked out and the food placed in the heated oven. Heat given off by the thick walls does the cooking.

In type number four, the Chinese oven, the fire is also built on the floor of the oven, but it is not removed when the food is put in place. The meat is suspended well above the fire in a short chimney, where it is cooked by the double action of the super-heated air rising from the fire and the heat radiating from the masonry walls.

Manufactured portable and permanent barbecues

There is a rapidly increasing variety of both portable and permanent manufactured barbecue units on the market. Innovations in barbecues have brought to the public many new shapes, sizes, colors, and types of barbecues that are easy to install and use, and require little or no maintenance.

Portable barbecue units. The simplest type of portable unit is the *"hibachi."* This is a table-top model, usually of cast construction, that has one, two, or three small grills side-by-side. The "hibachi" normally has three notches on the back into which the grills can be slipped for height adjustments. There are other short-legged table-top barbecues that have circular and rectangular grill shapes.

The *bowl-type* is one of the most familiar portable barbecues. This consists of a circular steel bowl supported by three detachable legs. A circular grill is mounted on an adjustable center post that may be raised or lowered relative to the coals contained in the bowl. Various attachments are available to make spit barbecuing and shish kebab cooking possible. With the addition of a sheet metal hood, the coals can be protected from the wind, retaining a large portion of the heat. This type of hood is often built with a warming shelf, front cover, spit supports, and a thermometer. *Note:* The life of the bowl can be extended by placing foil in the bowl and covering it with about 2 inches of pea gravel.

The *cart-type* barbecue unit can be the most elaborate of the portable barbecues. With serving counters and hoods that completely enclose the grill, almost any type of barbecuing can be achieved on the cart-type unit. Most of these rely on charcoal fuel, but some are equipped with electric heating elements, and others have gas burners.

Permanent barbecue units. There are also several new permanent, quick-installation barbecues on the market. Some indoor types can be easily installed in a kitchen counter. Other outdoor models are constructed for mounting on a single metal post in the selected barbecue area. These are primarily gas fired, but some are provided with electric heating elements. Gas or electricity is run to the unit, making barbecuing possible without the fuss of charcoal. This outdoor type is often manufactured with a hinged hood so smoke cooking is possible as well as ordinary grilling. Manufacturers claim that some of these new gas and electric units are capable of producing the same quality of barbecue taste as charcoal. (For more information on indoor barbecue units, see pages 32-37).

CART-STYLE BARBECUE is easily moved around the yard; has electric spit and hood.

PERMANENT GAS-FIRED UNIT is mounted on single pole; includes hood and removable cutting board.

Simple Outdoor Grills

TABLE EXTENSION for simple brick grill is made of 2-inch cedar planks.

CONTOURED BARBECUE-FIREPIT has top screen for grilling; second screen below holds coals.

No matter what the size or shape, a simple outdoor barbecue grill can perform the basic functions of barbecuing without straining the owner's pocketbook and without "shouting down" the patio's other landscape features.

You will find that simple outdoor grills can range from the classic masonry structures to the newer types of manufactured metal units (both permanent and portable).

The traditional barbecue is designed to burn charcoal. However, some modern barbecue units have electric grills. One manufactured model is supported off of the ground in the patio area by a single pipe, through which gas is pumped to the burners.

Masonry barbecues may be found casually inserted in a retaining wall, freestanding within the yard, or next to the house. Often these simple grills are paired with storage cupboards and counter space.

GAS-FIRED manufactured barbecue rests on single pipe which houses the fuel line.

*STATIONARY GRILLS rest on brick extensions
below surface level on opposite sides of counter.*

*EFFECTIVE LIGHTING makes outdoor
barbecue an inviting place for guests
to gather after dark. This masonry
model has a drop-in electric grill.*

BRICK WALL FORMS background for this
rustic brick barbecue; counter tops are stone.

INSET EFFECT is created by the dense
ivy surrounding this simple brick barbecue.

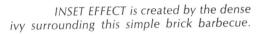

U-SHAPED WALL of burnt adobe encloses barbecue
and fuel supplies; lets chef face guests. Counter space
is plentiful for food preparation.

BARBECUE FOR A CROWD

A barbecue for 25 is almost as easy as one for just the family when you cook it on this big portable grill.

Because the grill can be raised or lowered on its fence-post supports to control the amount of heat reaching the grill, you can cook large meat cuts slowly and evenly.

This type of grill has the added advantage of being portable. When taken apart, it stores flat, and transports easily to the picnic site.

How to make the grill

For the legs you will need four 6-foot lengths of lightweight steel fence post that have self-fastening lugs at 6-inch intervals. For the grill, buy a 2 by 3-foot piece of heavy expanded steel and two 3-foot lengths of punched angle iron for edging.

Fasten angle irons (three bolts on each side will do it) onto the grill to give it extra strength and to make a protective edge along the sharp side of the steel. Cut four lengths of wire each about 12 inches long; at each corner of the grill, loop a piece of wire through the end hole of the angle iron and fasten it securely.

At the barbecue site, set the assembled grill on the ground and pound in a fence post about 2 inches out from each corner, making sure that the lugs on the posts are facing out. Lift the grill, slip the wire loops over the tops of the posts, and hang the loops on the lugs at the desired height.

BOLT ANGLE IRON to grill sides for reinforcement, and for protection from the sharp edges.

POUND STEEL POSTS into ground about two inches out from each corner of grill. Lugs face outward.

HANG GRILL from lugs at desired height above coals or fire; serving-basting tools also hang on lugs.

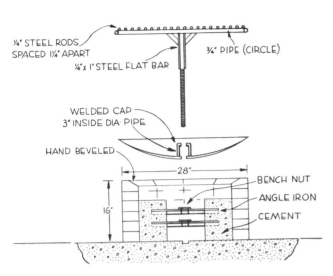

¼" STEEL RODS
SPACED 1¼" APART

¼" x 1" STEEL FLAT BAR

¾" PIPE (CIRCLE)

WELDED CAP
3" INSIDE DIA. PIPE

HAND BEVELED

28"

16"

BENCH NUT

ANGLE IRON

CEMENT

DISC FROM PLOW is pan for coals on this simple round barbecue unit. To raise the grill, you rotate it like a piano stool.

BARBECUE-FIREPLACE combination has plenty of counter space with storage underneath; spit or grill fits next to hot plate; and bricks in front of coals can be removed when cleaning firebox.

ROUGH STONE AND WOOD are combined to form barbecue-counter-cabinet. Electric rotisserie is removable to allow use of grill. Crank at right corner of grill raises and lowers the grate.

GRILL OR HOT PLATE height is adjusted by inserting it in the joints between bricks.

SUNKEN MASONRY BARBECUE is simply made; blends attractively with lines of yard.

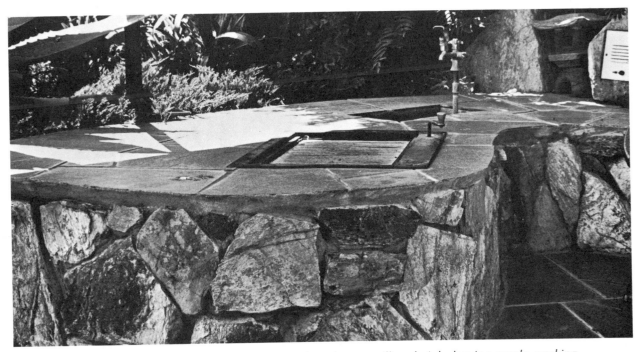

LOW LEVEL STONEWORK COUNTER is large enough to house grill and sink, leaving ample working space for food preparation. This barbecue unit forms a pleasing transition between patio area and garden.

A ROLL AROUND BARBECUE

This convenient approach to barbecuing combines a pair of hibachis with a child's wagon—the result is a barbecue with working space that will roll anywhere.

The wagon should be about 36 inches long—either the wood type shown here, or the more common metal type. Adapt the long dimension of the barbecue counter for a loose fit inside the wagon. The five spaced 2 by 2's at each end should give it about the right width; if it is more than 1/2 inch off, notch it or block the lower ends of the legs to fit. A metal wagon has rounded corners; if you are using one, cut off the four corner legs at the height of the wagon sides so those legs will fit over the corners.

You can use 3/4 inch plywood for the top. Cut holes in the top to fit your hibachis, and trim the edges with aluminum linoleum molding to reflect heat. After the top is attached, secure some pins or small wood blocks on the shelf to prevent the hibachis from sliding about when the cart moves.

Notch the two hardwood dowel handles to fit flat on the 2 by 2 rails, and slant their bolts as shown so they will be easy to grasp.

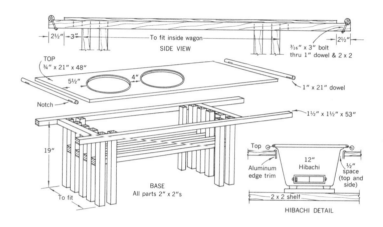

MATERIALS for mobile barbecue are readily available at hardware and lumber stores, and construction is simple. Hibachis may be taken out and used separately.

BARBECUE CART contains two hibachis, rolls easily over patio and lawn. Wagon bed serves as storage shelf; dowel handles serve as towel bars.

COUNTER AND STAND simply slip in and out of a child's wagon, require no bolting down or support. Both are easily cleaned and stored.

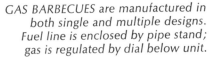

GAS BARBECUES are manufactured in both single and multiple designs. Fuel line is enclosed by pipe stand; gas is regulated by dial below unit.

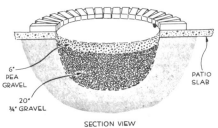

6"
PEA
GRAVEL

20"
¾" GRAVEL

PATIO
SLAB

SECTION VIEW

FIREPIT IN CONCRETE PATIO provides friendly gathering place for guests. Circle is made of Roman bricks set in mortar. Barbecuers use long-handled forks.

Open-Air Cooking Areas

LARGE HOOD carries off smoke from grill portion of complete outdoor cooking facility.

COOKING WALL of brick offers storage, sink, and charcoal grill in cozy patio corner.

Simple grills such as those shown in the preceding chapters will fill the basic barbecue needs of most households—particularly when the homeowner's yard is not large. To some families, however, the outdoor barbecue area is worthy of full emphasis, and they plan it boldly.

There are situations that lend themselves to the construction of a large barbecue structure around which the outdoor activities of the family may be centered.

Many outdoor kitchens include grills, spit attachments, ovens, sinks, storage, refrigerator units, electric appliances, and in some areas, fireplaces. If you decide to build this type of unit, it is wise to choose a site where the size of the barbecue will be in scale with surrounding trees, shrubs, and garden walls. Above all, remember that if you ever decide to sell your house, this "all-out" barbecue area can either be an asset or a liability—depending greatly upon its appearance.

WOODY ATMOSPHERE is emphasized by wooden barbecue buffet counter, deck, and fence.

CHARCOAL GRILL and sink are set in mosaic counter of freestanding barbecue.

PATIO KITCHEN is complete with refrigerator, barbecue, electric range, and smoke oven. Design and ceramic tile offer a hint of Spain.

BARBECUE AND OVEN-RANGE use gas, flexible fuel lines attach to outlets behind counter (see below). The appliances are mounted on casters and roll behind cabinet doors when not in use.

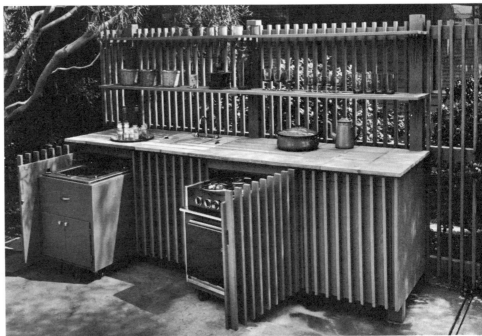

TWO SIMPLE OUTDOOR KITCHENS

Just about everything needed for barbecuing is kept in these two simple outdoor kitchens. When not used to store utensils, they become simple, convenient work areas for outdoor cooking.

The kitchen at left below is made of redwood stained to match the house siding. The equipment inside is kept dry partly because of the cabinet itself, and partly because it is under the roof overhang.

The barbecue center at right below is made of exterior plywood, attached to the house studs with six lag screws, and painted on the outside to match the house wall.

The cupboard is 6½ feet long, 4 feet high, 1⅓ feet deep. The two upper doors (16 by 34 inches) become counters when dropped down on chains held by screw eyes. Magnetic catches hold them when closed.

SIDE OF HOUSE supports handy cabinet containing hibachi and all of the necessary utensils and fuel.

UTENSILS, FUEL, AND SPICES are at arm's length; chain holds shelves horizontal for counter space.

Indoor-Outdoor Barbecues

GENEROUS-SIZED fireplace-barbecue
combination is protected by patio overhead.

USED BRICK enhances large barbecue unit in
outdoor room; storage is plentiful.

A barbecue installed in a lanai, roofed patio, or a recessed porch, meets all the tests for an ideally located unit: It is sheltered from the weather, it forms the center of an outdoor living area, and is usually easily accessible to the kitchen. And, if you live in an area where you can combine the barbecue with a fireplace, you will have a warm, friendly spot where family and guests can congregate on cool days and evenings.

An indoor-outdoor installation does not have to be built at the time a new house is constructed, nor does it have to fit a particular style of architecture. Most units can be attractively adapted to almost any situation.

For those who have ample room away from the house, an enclosed barbecue retreat may be built for comfortable barbecuing year-round. It may be anything from a simple arbor sheltered by vines to a roofed outdoor room. (For ideas on roofing materials, see the *Sunset* book, *How to Build Patio Roofs.)*

LANAI BARBECUE has pass-through to indoor kitchen at the right of grill.

HOOD is effective for long, slow barbecuing; three sections are removable.

UPRIGHT FIREBOX is for spit roasting; hooks hold meat for smoke cooking.

RECESSED BETWEEN FIREPLACE and kitchen window, indoor-outdoor barbecue backs up against grillework that allows filtered view of trees beyond. Kitchen window can be opened to provide pass-through.

COMBINATION BARBECUE and fireplace are constructed of ashlar-cut stone. Old-fashioned wood-burning stove is attractively built into structure at left. High temperature areas are lined with brick.

CANTILEVERED BARBECUE extends from brick house wall. Large hood carries smoke out of covered patio area.

BARBECUE-BUFFET ROLLS OUT

Like a large piece of built-in furniture, this buffet wraps around an outside corner of the house and becomes part of the architecture.

The sides and front of the buffet are constructed from the same grooved, rough-sawn siding as the exterior walls of the house. The counter-top is laminated plastic.

For daily use, the buffet—held against the wall with simple hook-eye fasteners—serves the purpose of any countertop.

When it's time to entertain, however, it rolls away from the wall on large heavy-duty rubber casters to serve as a barbecue center and buffet counter. The inside is divided into two long shelves for storage.

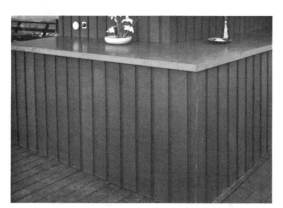

STORED against walls, counter blends with siding.

BUFFET rolls away from house walls for serving.

STAINLESS STEEL UNIT is recessed in wall of outdoor room. When not in use, folding doors close in front of it. Shish kebab skewers are gang-rotated by electric motor inside the barbecue; can be replaced with a grill. Barbecue is gas-fired.

GLASS DOORS of stone barbecue can be closed to confine heat from coals and restrict smoke to chimney.

Indoor Barbecue Grills

OFF DINING AREA, barbecue-fireplace is
built in adobe wall. Metalwork is wrought steel.

KITCHEN ISLAND has gas-fired barbecue
across from range; fan in hood serves both.

Thanks to indoor barbecue grills many families are able to enjoy barbecued food all year around giving no thought to weather conditions.

Two of the most popular styles of indoor grills are: 1) those built out from the wall and vented through an overhead hood, and 2) those built into small raised fireplaces. Either style may be located in the kitchen, dining room, family room, or recreation room.

One comparatively new idea—the kitchen counter-top grill—is especially popular with homeowners who like their barbecues to be inconspicuous. One model is equipped with a fan which pulls smoke and grease down through the electric grill and grease filter, and vents the smoke and odors through the side of the house.

The gas-fired indoor grill has become quite popular in many households. Proponents argue that if you're going to have a gas line for ignition anyway, the rapid heating, close control, and tidiness of a gas fire compensate for the loss of fireplace fun that goes with charcoal cookery. Electric heating elements also share most of these qualities.

MEXICAN TILE and copper surround barbecue with intriguing results.

HINGED HOODS set down over double grills to contain heat and smoke for cooking. Unit fits attractively into cooking wall in combination kitchen-dining room.

GARDEN ROOM opens to patio through sliding glass doors that visually extend space within the room. Combination fireplace-barbecue has generous all-purpose cabinet storage space below.

ELECTRIC GRILL-STOVE combination is tucked into kitchen alcove. Hood is hidden behind paneling.

COUNTER-TOP GRILL is heated electrically. Fan vents smoke to outside and draws grease down into filter.

STRATEGICALLY LOCATED between dining room and family room, this counter high grill is an important food preparation center. Tile-top hearth is easy to clean.

VENTILATION HOOD for this indoor charcoal barbecue is hidden in cupboard above.

CERAMIC TILE set into adobe wall is attractive surrounding for electric grill.

IS CHARCOAL BEST?

Will the meat broiled over a gas-fired grill taste as good as meat broiled over glowing coals? Many claim that it does.

Often, gas-fired barbecue units have a layer of light-weight lava rock interposed between the gas burners and the grill. This rock, heated by the gas burners, radiates heat in much the same way as charcoal coals. Grease dripping from the meat during the broiling process drops on the heated lava rocks; there it sears and burns, imparting barbecue taste odors to the meat. Dampened hickory chips can also be placed over the rocks to give additional hickory flavor to the meat in the same manner as would be done over a charcoal fire.

Caution: Charcoal should not be burned indoors without proper ventilation, as the carbon monoxide it produces can be fatal.

GLASS DOORS are paired with metal storage doors in this indoor dressed-stone unit.

GRILL LIFTS OFF this manufactured unit so skewers can be set across coals.

Smoke Ovens and Pit Barbecues

BARBECUF PIT serves 300 to 600 persons; is built along same lines as plan on page 79.

JAPANESE SMOKE OVEN, called a kamado, is built into outdoor buffet counter.

Many people prefer the definite smoky flavor of smoke-cooked food to that of food prepared on a spit or grill. The taste of smoke-cooked food leaves no doubt that it was cooked over a fire of coals. The two most common ways of preparing food in this manner are the Chinese oven and the deep pit barbecue.

When using a Chinese smoke oven, a fire is built at the bottom of the firebox an hour or so before the cooking is to commence. The meat is suspended well above the fire—generally within the area of a short chimney.

The deep-pit barbecue oven is similar to the Chinese oven, only it is underground. A deep hole is dug in the ground and often lined with brick—the walls of this hole serve as the oven. A fire is started at the bottom of the pit, and when plenty of coals are formed, meat is suspended half way down the hole (often along with fruit and vegetables). The hole is then covered with boards and sealed until the food is cooked.

WOODEN BARREL is smoke oven; rods for hanging food rest in notches of steel bars.

IMMENSELY PRACTICAL Chinese oven has seat that also provides convenient step. Firebox is outside oven.

SHEET METAL HOOD controls draft at top. Fowl and ribs can be hung from hooks at top.

LOOSE-TEXTURED FOOD is placed on hardware cloth, then set on built-in grill.

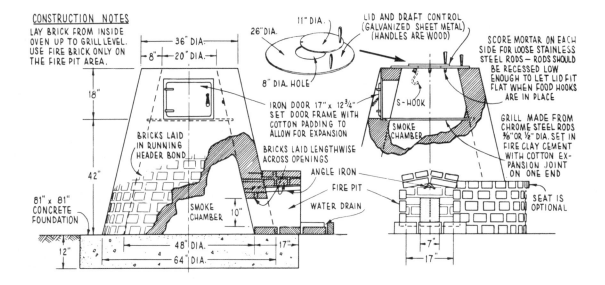

CONSTRUCTION NOTES
LAY BRICK FROM INSIDE OVEN UP TO GRILL LEVEL. USE FIRE BRICK ONLY ON THE FIRE PIT AREA.

36" DIA.
8" 20" DIA.
18"
42"
81" x 81" CONCRETE FOUNDATION
12"
48" DIA.
64" DIA.

BRICKS LAID IN RUNNING HEADER BOND
SMOKE CHAMBER
10"

26" DIA.
11" DIA.
8" DIA. HOLE

LID AND DRAFT CONTROL (GALVANIZED SHEET METAL) (HANDLES ARE WOOD)

IRON DOOR 17" x 12¾" SET DOOR FRAME WITH COTTON PADDING TO ALLOW FOR EXPANSION
BRICKS LAID LENGTHWISE ACROSS OPENINGS
ANGLE IRON
FIRE PIT
WATER DRAIN

SCORE MORTAR ON EACH SIDE FOR LOOSE STAINLESS STEEL RODS — RODS SHOULD BE RECESSED LOW ENOUGH TO LET LID FIT FLAT WHEN FOOD HOOKS ARE IN PLACE

S-HOOK
SMOKE CHAMBER

GRILL MADE FROM CHROME STEEL RODS ⅜" OR ½" DIA. SET IN FIRE CLAY CEMENT WITH COTTON EXPANSION JOINT ON ONE END

SEAT IS OPTIONAL

7"
17"

A BARBECUE FOR HUNDREDS

Here is how to barbecue enough meat for feeding 600 persons:

Dig a pit about 16 feet long, 8 feet deep, and 8 feet wide. Cover the bottom with cobblestones or firebricks, and build an oak fire on this base. After six hours, the coals should be ready for cooking. Hang a heavy wire netting half way down the pit; place the meat (cut roast size) on the matting. Lay wooden planks across the top, snugly-butted together. Cover these with heavy canvas and seal the edge of the canvas and any steam jets with a layer of dirt. Let the meat roast for about 6 hours. This pit has a capacity for two prime beef two-year-old steers when prepared for barbecuing.

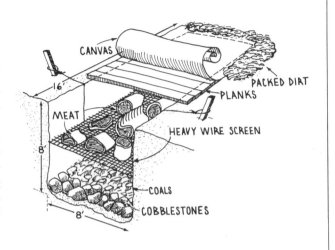

ELEGANTLY APPOINTED whisky barrel has copper lining, and electric spit attachment. The grill for this smoke oven is supported above the fire pan which is set on a winch-operated platform.

VERSATILE SMOKE OVEN can be used in three different ways: as a regular barbecue (note that grill is in place), as a firepit (with grill removed), or as a smoke oven (with food hung in chimney).

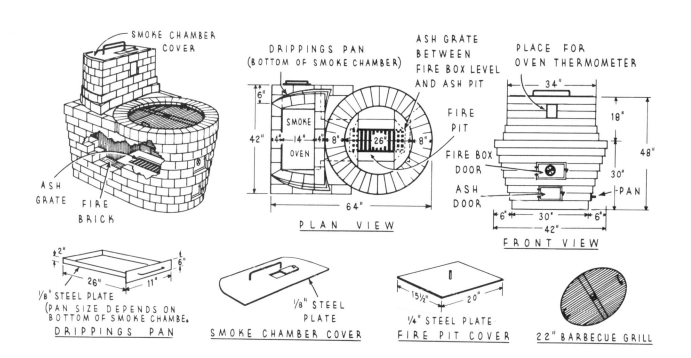

SMOKE CHAMBER COVER

ASH GRATE

FIRE BRICK

DRIPPINGS PAN (BOTTOM OF SMOKE CHAMBER)

SMOKE OVEN

6"

42"

4" 14" 8"

64"

PLAN VIEW

ASH GRATE BETWEEN FIRE BOX LEVEL AND ASH PIT

FIRE PIT

FIRE BOX DOOR

ASH DOOR

26"

8"

PLACE FOR OVEN THERMOMETER

34"

18"

48"

30"

PAN

6" 30" 6"

42"

FRONT VIEW

2"

6"

26" 11"

1/8" STEEL PLATE (PAN SIZE DEPENDS ON BOTTOM OF SMOKE CHAMBE.

DRIPPINGS PAN

1/8" STEEL PLATE

SMOKE CHAMBER COVER

15½" 20"

1/4" STEEL PLATE

FIRE PIT COVER

22" BARBECUE GRILL

SMOKE A TURKEY UNDER A HOOD OF FOIL

You can convert a simple barbecue into an effective smoke oven that can handle the largest chicken or turkey you can buy. It takes only some wire and a 25-foot roll of heavy aluminum foil for making a dome.

The foil dome, by enclosing hot smoke from the fire, imparts a mild smoke flavor to the fowl at the same time that it reflects the heat back for cooking. This combination can give you an exceptionally well-flavored and beautifully browned turkey.

Once the fire is started, and with the barbecue in a convenient place near the kitchen, you can watch and baste the turkey almost as easily as if it were in a regular oven. A foil pan under the turkey collects the drippings for gravy.

How to make the dome

First shape a wire frame to whatever size is needed. The barbecue shown is 24 inches in diameter; for this one, use 7 feet of 5-gage wire, 16 feet of 10-gage wire, and a small roll of 22-gage wire (all galvanized steel).

With the 5-gage wire, form a base ring to fit inside the barbecue rim. Whip the ring's ends together with the fine 22-gage wire. Then use four 4-foot lengths of 10-gage wire bowed across the ring to form a dome about 16-inches high. Twist the ends (several turns) around the base ring. Whip wires together at the top with 22-gage wire.

To cover the dome: Tear lengths of heavy metal foil from a roll, each 5 inches longer than the arc from the dome's base to its peak. Lay the strips side by side, with shiny sides up. Seam them securely together by holding two edges together (dull side facing dull side) and folding a 1/2-inch edge over and over several times. In this way, make a continuous blanket of foil long enough to encircle the base ring, and allow about 2 extra inches for joining ends.

Lay the wire frame on its side on top of the foil with the base ring about 1 inch from one of the long sides of the foil. Turn edge of foil over base ring, rolling ring as you work, until the two ends of the foil meet; join as you did the other seams. Carefully pleat the foil between seams to shape it to the frame. Grasp foil at center top and twist together to make a handle.

For making the drip pan, use a double thickness of the foil. Fold and crease corners to shape into shallow pans. With a center support in the barbecue, it is necessary to make two pans to fit on either side of the post.

SIMPLE BARBECUE is converted into smoke oven by covering wire frame with foil, making foil drip-pan (secured in place with paper clips), and preparing separate fires on either side of pan.

Metal Fixtures and Accessories

There are many manufacturers who produce excellent metal equipment designed expressly for barbecues. Many of them make the full range of needed accessories: grills and grates (both stationary and elevating), spits, hot plates, ovens, and doors. Each manufacturer, however, has worked out his own refinements that distinguish his line from his competitors'. These differences may be important to your planned installation, and you would be wise to obtain catalogues and price lists for several lines for comparison and study. You can get manufacturers' names from the classified telephone directory (look under "Barbecue Equipment"), from garden supply centers, hardware stores, or masonry contractors.

Perhaps most important, manufacturers' lists will provide you with the dimensions of the items that interest you. The sizes of grills and grates are fairly well standardized, but most makers figure their dimensions from brick size, and there are different-sized bricks and various ways of arranging them around an opening. *It is safest to select your grill unit and spit cooking accessories first and then fit your barbecue around it afterward.*

Selecting the grill

The ideal grill should be sturdy enough to withstand heat and to support a load of food and utensils without sagging and yet be light enough to handle easily. It should be detachable so you can easily get at the coals, remove it from the flames while you are burning wood down to charcoal,

and take it out for storing between seasons. It should be easy to keep clean and free of rust.

Grills are made from various kinds of iron and steel. A popular material is steel rod, used either in 3/16-inch size or smaller, set about an inch apart in a frame. These rods are often chrome plated to protect them against rust. Another popular metal is a lightweight mesh known as "expanded metal." The steel is about 1/8 inch in thickness, formed into open diamond shapes 3/4 by 1 1/2 inches. This mesh is lightweight but surprisingly strong and its form tends to dissipate the heat and prevent warping.

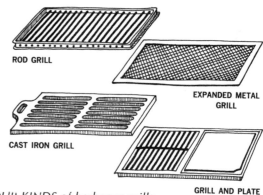

ROD GRILL

EXPANDED METAL GRILL

CAST IRON GRILL

GRILL AND PLATE

FOUR KINDS of barbecue grills.

Cast iron also is used to a certain extent. This material is slow to heat, but once it is warmed up, it retains heat longer than other metals. It is heavy and brittle, but with care should outlast the barbecue. Most expensive, but perhaps most trouble-free, is stainless steel. Available in either rod or mesh form, it doesn't rust and it can be used in lighter gauges than regular steel. It costs five or six times more than regular steel.

Stationary grills. The least expensive grill obtainable is the type that is simply placed loose on top of the firepit. When paired with an immovable grate, it is difficult to learn to use, because it requires complete mastery of the barbecue fire. However, many barbecuers prefer it to movable types.

Stationary grills are obtainable in several sizes, mostly scaled to fit loosely inside brickwork. Standard dimensions are:

12 inches by 16, 18, or 22 inches
15 inches by 18 or 22 inches
16 inches by 20, 24, or 28 inches
18 inches by 24, 30, or 36 inches

If you need a bigger grill than the largest one listed above, get two smaller ones. There is a limit to the distance a grill can span without sagging under load. Many of the grills sold singly by manufacturers fit into elevating devices that they also market. If you intend to invest in such an assembly later, make certain that it will fit your firebox.

Simplest method of installing a fixed grill is to rest it on top of the firebox. However, because it can be easily dislodged, it is better to install it below the top on a ledge of projecting bricks. If you

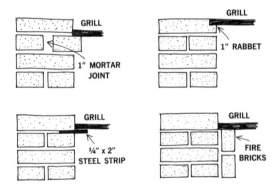

FOUR WAYS of setting stationary grill in place.

like to do things the hard way, chip out a rabbet in the top row of bricks on each side of the firebox and rest the grill in the grooves. Or, you can support it on an iron strip set in the mortar between two courses of bricks. A quarter-inch flat bar, 2 inches wide, should be satisfactory. Set it 1½ inches inside the mortar. Some equipment manufacturers make a frame that fits around the rim of the firepit and supports the grill on an inside flange. *Whatever way you choose, don't cement the grill in place.*

Grates for the fire

The shelf for centering the fire under the grill is usually made of either brick or metal. Though brick fireshelves often outlast the metal because clay brick is less affected by concentrated heat than is metal, the metal types are very popular.

The ideal metal grate is one that won't burn out quickly, that functions efficiently, and yet is light enough to lift easily. Cast iron is the traditional material for grates. It stands up well under fire, in fact, fire hardens it, and it can be cast in patterns of proven efficiency. But it is heavy and brittle and thus should be used only for grates that do not have to be handled often.

A quarter-inch boiler plate is popular for solid fireshelves. If the surface area of the plate is large, the grate is likely to warp from the intense heat of the coals unless it is protected to some degree. A polka-dot pattern of ¾-inch holes, drilled an inch or so apart, will tend to disperse the expansion evenly and prevent or reduce warping. A layer of brick placed over the metal will also lengthen its life.

Grates should never be cemented in place. They should be set loosely in the structure so they can expand and contract freely and so they may be removed if replacement is ever necessary.

Although charcoal and hard woods leave a surprisingly small amount of ash, you should make certain that ashes do not gather on an exposed grate. Water from a garden sprinkler or a passing rain cloud will convert the ashes to lye, which has a hearty appetite for iron.

Elevating grills and grates

There are two popular devices obtainable that are designed to permit mechanical control of the barbecue fire. With one type, the grill is lowered to the coals; with the other the fire is brought up to the grill.

Elevating grills. The elevating grill assembly consists of a standard grill, fitted into a rack that is raised or lowered by a crank-driven mechanism. Advocates of this type point out that it permits use of a durable masonry fireshelf, that it is lighter and easier to raise and lower than a heavy firebasket, and that it permits cooking within the firebox, thus taking advantage of the sheltering radiance of the masonry walls. Also, it is more suitable for use with wood fuel than the elevating

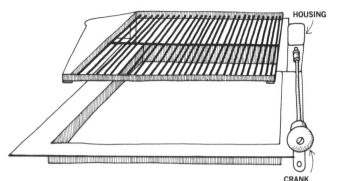

GRILL is raised, lowered by crank mechanism.

grate, which often does not have the necessary capacity to hold sticks of firewood.

Elevating grates. With the elevating grate device, the grill remains stationary while the coal basket is raised or lowered by a mechanism similar to that used with the elevating grill.

Those who favor the elevating grate contend that a lowered grill is awkward and hazardous to work with down in the fire pit, and they call attention to the fact that their grill is always stationary,

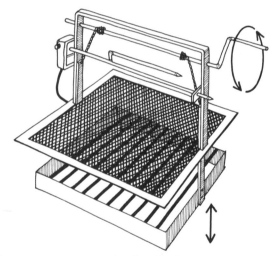

GRATE IS ELEVATED by hand; electric spit included.

like a kitchen stove top. They also note that this type eliminates any necessity for building a fire-shelf in the barbecue, thereby simplifying construction. They also point to the efficient design of the firebasket itself that admits air to the coals from below and all sides.

Sizes. Dimensions of either elevating grill or grate assemblies are usually given as the size of the pit openings that they fit, although some manufacturers list them by grill size. For dimensions of standard firebox openings, see pages 51-52.

If you buy an elevating grill, find out how far into the firebox it drops so you can provide room for an ample bed of coals on the grate. Most grills descend about 12 inches.

Check points. Whichever device you buy, try out the lifting mechanism and the brake that holds the grill or grate stationary, and see if they work simply and freely. You won't want to have to wrestle with it when it is operating over hot coals. Also, check

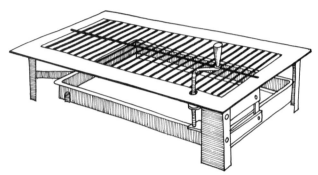

CRANK RAISES, lowers pan of coals; grill remains stationary; unit popular with indoor barbecues.

the provisions for attaching extras, such as revolving spit, revolving grill, skewers, and condiment shelf.

Installation. Most of these assemblies are easy to install. The majority are made with a flange or collar that fits around the inner rim of the firebox opening or a footing that stands on the floor of the firebox. They are simply set in place. Some are made so they slip like a drawer into a shelf-like firebox. Removed, they leave space for an open fire.

The revolving grill

The revolving grill consists, basically, of two grills that are clamped together and rotated by the motor used to drive the spit. It does an excellent grilling job with steaks, spare ribs, franks, fish, and half fowl, but it is very hot to handle when it comes time to unclamp the grills and remove the cooked food.

A vertical firebasket to save the drippings

A vertical firebasket is a useful companion to a spit. With this arrangement, coals are contained in an ironwork basket that is usually hung against the back wall of an indoor-type barbecue. Heat radiating from the fire cooks the meat revolving 4 to 6 inches in front of the coals. The great advantage of this device is that it permits the drippings from the spitted meat to be caught in a pan on the hearth and re-used for basting, instead of being wasted in the fire.

Hot plates—fixed and removable

The barbecue hot plate is a square of heavy metal that rests like a lid over the firepit, and converts the open-air grill to an outdoor stove. Properly put to work, it can diversify the range of barbecue cooking. It makes light work of fixing flapjacks or "ham-and-eggs," toasting buns or bread, or frying the greasy meats, such as lamb or sausage, that drop part of their flavor into the coals with their drippings. It also permits cooking without the flare-ups that often disturb the cook who is working over an open grill.

Hot plates are made of a variety of materials: cast iron, boiler plate, pickled iron, and cast aluminum. In general, the heavier the material the longer it will last, but if the plate is going to be exposed only occasionally, a light gauge is adequate. The barbecuer will probably find that a plate with a grease gutter or a raised lip may be easier to use than a clean-edged type, because it will not shed molten fat into the fire.

Fixed installations. Hot plates are obtainable in several sizes and styles. The largest ones seal the entire top opening of the firebox and are usually hinged or attached permanently in place. They can only be used with a chimney that vents the smoke and gases from the burning fuel. If their surface area is too great they are difficult to heat uniformly—an egg will cook instantaneously on one spot of the plate or loll around indifferently in another. Also, if an all-over plate is constantly exposed to fire, it will buckle in time. Some hot plates are hard to clean: the bottom surface becomes sooted over, the top side rusty. And unless they have a built-in grease gutter, they drain hot fat onto the masonry walls.

Removable types. Removable hot plates are popular because they are easily cleaned and they can be set in place or removed according to the needs of the cook. They are available in sizes ranging from full grill-size to small plates just big enough to hold a pair of hot cakes. The larger sizes are designed either to fit into the frame that holds the grill or to rest on top of the grill itself. Some of

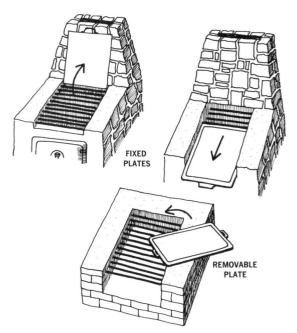

FIXED HOT PLATES require chimney; others do not.

those that fit into the grill frame are made the same size as the grill, for which they may be substituted as necessary; and some occupy half the space, sharing the frame equally with a companion grill. If you plan to buy an all-over plate, make certain that it won't close off the draft to the fire. There should be an inch or two clearance between the outer edge of the plate and the wall of the firebox.

Spits—electric and manual

Some experienced barbecuers can successfully cook roasts and whole fowl right on the grill. But, most outdoor cooks find it simpler to rely on a revolving spit, installed over the firebox.

The typical barbecue spit is a pointed steel rod, on which the meat is impaled, with attachments to keep it from twisting around. The spit is rested in a bearing cradle on each side of the firebox and rotated by hand or by machine. A metal counter balance is an essential accessory when you are cooking heavy meats and fowl; by preventing undue strain, it will insure a longer life for your motor.

Types to choose from. The barbecue builder can select from quite an assortment of spits. These types range from a simple skewer that any boy could make in a metal shop to intricate models that keep two dozen birds rotating over a sea of coals. They are made to fit various types of installations: some slip into brackets rested on the rim of the firepit, some clamp to the frame for the grill elevating mechanism, and others are made to be set anywhere, over the barbecue grill or a firepit or inside a fireplace. They are obtainable in either stainless steel or plain steel, painted or chrome-plated.

Rotation of the spit. The secret of thorough spit cooking is rotation of the meat at a pace that insures even exposure to the coals. Two types of motive power are used to turn spits: electric motors and the human hand. The hand-operated types (rapidly becoming scarce in this mechanized age) are provided with a locking device so the spit can be held in any one of several positions. You simply advance the handle a quarter turn every now and then and fix a fresh surface of the meat over the heat. Since spit cooking is a long-drawn-out affair —a roast takes from 2 to 4 hours—hand-turning is a confining and monotonous chore. Most cooks gladly consign this job to an electric motor.

Shish kebab attachments

The small brothers of the barbecue spit, shish kebab skewers are a popular and versatile addition to any barbecue. They consist of long, thin pointed shafts that are laid across the firepit after being loaded with alternating cubes of meat and savory bits of bacon, tomato, pineapple, or whatever appeals to the venturesome cook. They may also be employed for more humble service, such as toasting wienies, buns, or roasting corn. Shish kebab skewers are obtainable in plain or stainless steel, with or without handles. Some are made up in multiple units, gang-rotated by an electric motor.

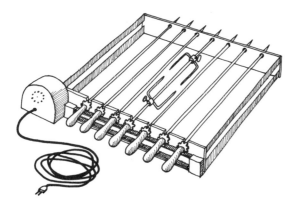

SHISH KEBAB SKEWERS are electrically rotated.

Doors for barbecue unit

Metal doors are installed in barbecues to perform specialized functions. They are used to control draft, give access to the fire, permit ash removal, close an oven or incinerator, and cover storage

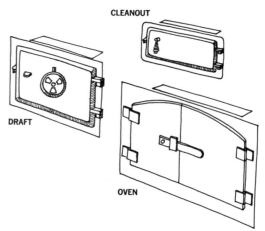

BARBECUE DOORS control draft, permit easy removal of ashes, retain oven heat, and open to storage.

compartments. Although specially-designed doors are available for each of these functions, one or two all-purpose doors can be used for any or all of these operations. Many of the doors sold for barbecues are actually furnace closures that have been on the market for a generation or two.

Draft doors. Set into the wall of the firebox at grate-level, draft doors permit control over the fire. They allow the barbecuer to reach in and tame the coals or to adjust the draft by leaving the door ajar or by fiddling with a spinner in its center.

Their installation is partly a matter of personal option. As a draft source, they are not absolutely essential, for enough air usually passes through the grill opening to keep a suitable bed of coals alive. They are sometimes helpful in providing an extra draft when the fire is just starting, but once the fire has caught, their main value is in providing access rather than draft to the fire.

A draft door is a great convenience in an installation that requires direct manipulation of the coals for maintenance of cooking temperatures, as it is with a grill that cannot be removed quickly when access to the fire is necessary.

Clean-out doors. Clean-out doors are installed in the base of a barbecue or incinerator to give access to the ash pit. An opening left in the bottom courses of brick work will do just as well for a barbecue, although a door will prevent ashes from blowing out and small animals from moving in.

Oven doors. These come singly or attached to a fabricated oven unit. Since many builders now use a large-size flue tile for the oven proper, the unattached door should do for most installations. Either cast iron or steel is usable. Many draft doors are adaptable as closures for small-sized ovens. Check with your local dealer for available types and sizes.

Storage doors. King-size steel doors are used to close large openings, such as the face of a fuel or utensil cabinet. They may be made from scrap iron or they may be purchased from manufacturers. Many builders prefer to use wood for storage doors not subjected to heat because it is cheaper, lighter, and easier to work than steel. If you are interested in steel storage doors, it is best to check dimensions with manufacturers, as they are not standardized.

Installation. Barbecue doors are easily installed. They come hinged to frames that are scaled to fit into openings in brick work. The frames are equipped with flanges that slip into the mortar joints and hold the door rigid and at the same time support the surrounding masonry. Except for very large ones exposed to heat, they do not require an allowance for expansion, and the frames may be set snugly in place.

Normal procedure calls for propping the door in place and building the brick work around it. This is a wise trade practice, because doors, like bricks, come in a variety of shapes and sizes, and their fitting often calls for increasing or decreasing the size of the mortar joints in the surrounding courses of brick.

Doors are commonly listed in trade catalogues by their actual dimensions, rather than the size of the opening they are made to fit. The sizes most easily obtained are: 6x9, 8x10, 10x12, 12x14, 14x16. As a rule, these would fit openings about 1/2 inch smaller in each dimension.

Barbecue doors are available in a choice of hinge positions. Most are hinged at the side, either left or right; a few open at the top or bottom. The choice between left and right-hand swing is strictly a question of the working convenience in your particular installation. Avoid a bottom-hinged door. These shin-crackers are awkward to handle, and some of the cast iron varieties tend to snap their hinges if allowed to drop open.

Metal hoods

Metal hoods are commonly installed over indoor grills to direct smoke and combustion gases up the flue. To insure proper draw and to protect you and your guests from being "smoked out," it is important that a fan be included within the interior of the hood.

Although hoods are often made up by local metal shops to architects' specifications, they are also produced by some barbecue equipment makers in a selection of metals and a choice of sizes scaled to standard fireplace widths. They are made with a flange along the top edge that may be embedded in a running mortar joint. Obtainable in stainless steel, or in black, bronze, and copper finishes.

COPPER HOOD is 18 inches above counter barbecue grill; draws smoke and cooking odors.

Basic Construction Specifications

Before you start to plan or build an actual barbecue unit, you will find it advisable to fortify yourself with some knowledge of the accepted requirements for its principal parts, such as the foundation, firebox, fireplace, and chimney.

The right foundation

If your climate is frostless and your soil is compact sand or hard clay, well drained, you can get by without a special foundation. But if the conditions differ, your barbecue will require a substantial base.

A poor weight-bearing soil, such as adobe, loam, or loose sand, will settle, swell, or sluice away when wet, and almost any type of soil will heave and buckle during prolonged freezing spells. The most treacherous building surface is fresh fill of any type soil. Don't construct a barbecue on it unless your architect or a qualified engineer works out the foundation details.

A good foundation permits the soil to move around without straining the barbecue structure and causing it to split open. It ties the barbecue together into a unit that will ride the ground swells like a boat. At worst, after a severe winter, a well-footed barbecue may develop a slight list when the soil dries out. But this can be corrected by jacking up the low end with a house jack and filling in with concrete.

Sometimes, the foundation needs protection from sub-surface water. If your site does not drain naturally, provide a porous gravel pad 6 to 8 inches thick for the foundation to rest upon. For a hillside site, extend the gravel bed along the up-side of the foundation to prevent water from damming behind it.

Direct footing. If soil and climatic conditions permit you to do without a foundation, you should start the barbecue wall below the surface to insure a firm bed. Dig a trench through the cultivated top soil, down about 6 inches or until you reach hard ground. Level and tamp the bottom, soak it

DIG FOUNDATION BED 6" deep; level, tamp bottom.

thoroughly, and let it settle over night. Check and correct the level next day, then lay your brick or stone directly on the soil, or, if you prefer, on top of a 1½-inch compacted sand cushion.

Concrete slab. The most popular type of barbecue foundation is the reinforced concrete slab. For any but unusually heavy structures, a slab from 4 to 6 inches in depth makes a satisfactory base. In severe frost areas, the slab should be built down below the frost line or at least below the top foot of soil where the principal frost movement occurs.

A concrete slab requires reinforcement. Concrete won't "bend" and it is likely to fracture if subjected to a twisting, uneven load such as might come from a shift in the subsoil. Steel reinforcing rods, 1/4 to 1/2 inch in diameter, should be laid checkerboard fashion on 6 to 12-inch centers with the intersections wired together. A heavy wire matting will do just as well, and it is simpler to install if you can buy it cut to your dimensions. Ask for a 6-inch mesh of 10 to 16-gauge galvanized wire. Either rods or mesh should be set in place half way up the slab.

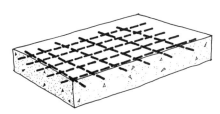

SLAB FOUNDATION should be 4 to 6 inches in depth.

Ideally, outside dimensions of the concrete slab should be at least 2 inches greater all around than the outside of the barbecue. While you're at it, you might extend the matte out in front to form a wide platform hearth or even a complete dining terrace.

Brick slab. If you prefer, you may build a slab foundation of reinforced bricks. This is an easy type to construct, and it eliminates the necessity for mixing concrete. However, a brick slab is more expensive than one made of concrete.

On the prepared earth or gravel bed, stand the bricks on edge in basket weave pattern, 1/2 inch apart. Prepare a thin mortar or grout (1 part cement, 1/4 part lime or fireclay, 3 parts sand) and pour in all the joints, filling them about half full.

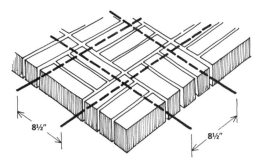

STEEL RODS set in joints reinforce brick slab.

Place 1/4 or 1/2-inch reinforcing rods in the open joints. Run them both ways at the change of pattern. Then fill up the joints with grout.

Continuous footing. For a large installation or one that requires a deep base, a foundation similar to the type used in home construction may be preferable to a concrete or brick slab. This is known as a continuous footing. It simply follows the shape of the barbecue walls, extending them well below the surface of the soil. It requires less excavation and less concrete than a slab carrying the same load. For an amateur, building this type of foundation is a rugged job because it calls for careful construction of wooden forms, tricky placement of reinforcing rods, and precise leveling all around when it is poured.

The continuous footing should extend 8 to 10 inches below grade (18" in frost areas) and run 6 inches in width for a single-brick wall, or 2 inches wider than the rocks used in a stone wall.

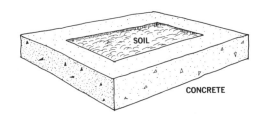

CONCRETE EXTENDS 8 to 10 inches below grade.

A continuous footing may also be made of bricks, simply by widening the base of the brick wall sufficiently to disperse the bearing pressure on the soil. Just build an 8-inch wall for two or three courses below grade, then start construction of the single-brick barbecue wall. If soil conditions are unstable, lay 1/4 to 3/8-inch reinforcing rods in the mortar joint between the first and second courses.

Firebox specifications

There are no hard and fast specifications for the barbecue firebox. The size of its top opening is determined by the dimensions of the grill you select; its depth, by the fuel you plan to use and the type of grill or grate you favor.

Top opening. The top opening is usually placed at counter-height (24-30 inches) and is lined up with its long side facing the barbecuer, enabling him to reach the back surface of the grill without singeing his shirt sleeves. The actual dimensions of the opening will depend upon the area of cooking surface you desire.

Most grills are made to fit inside brickwork. Three of the most popular sizes of firebox openings are: 19"x22½", 19"x26½", and 19"x32". However, sizes of grill units vary according to the manufacturer. The important thing to remember is this: *Select your grill unit first; then build your firebox so it will fit.*

Depth. The depth of the firebox is mainly determined by the type of grill and the kind of fuel you are using.

The floor of a firebox to be used with a stationary grill should be built from 6 to 9 inches below the grill for charcoal fuel, 9 to 12 inches below for hard wood.

For an elevating grill installation, leave room for the grill to descend to within a few inches of the coal bed. Thus, if your grill drops 8 inches, the grate floor should be set at least 10 inches below counter-height to allow for a 2-inch layer of coals. An elevating charcoal basket actually requires no firebox floor other than the foundation slab, but if it is used with a floored firebox, the coal basket should hang free at least 2 inches above the floor so air can reach its bottom surface.

The floor of the firebox proper can be made of various materials: cast iron grating, slotted to admit air from below and to sift ashes downward, or boiler plate (see page 45); earthen fill; or a layer of brick resting on fill or a supporting floor. If you install a metal floor, make provisions for its easy removal.

Outside facing. The face of the firebox may be constructed in one of three ways. Simplest is to leave the combustion area wide open in front. This provides generous draft and easy access to the coals, but it is a hot spot before which to work and it may shed sparks or a hot coal now and then.

At the other extreme, the fire chamber can be completely enclosed, or bricked-in with incidental provisions for draft, such as slots left open in the mortar joints or a brick or two omitted. This works quite well, providing the grill fits loosely enough so it doesn't choke off air to the coals when it is covered with food. An enclosed firebox is awkward to clear of ashes, which have to be scooped out from the top, unless it is coupled with an ash pit with a clean-out.

A compromise involves installation of a draft door in the firebox face. This permits the fire chamber to be left open or closed, according to the needs of the moment. The door may be opened to provide supplementary draft, to permit freshening of the fire, or to clean out an accumulation of ashes.

Ash pit. In some installations, the firebox has a lower compartment where the ashes gather. The only recommendation affecting the ash pit is to be sure to slant the floor so rain water will not collect there in winter. Ashes may be removed either through a door in front or an opening in the rear or side walls. Many designers feel that the ash pit is a waste of potential storage space. Instead, they prefer to install a solid floor under the coals and use the free space beneath for storing supplies or warming food.

The importance of a chimney

The only type of chimney that can cope with the smoke and combustion gases given off by a barbecue grill is one that is built directly overhead. The heat from the barbecue fire rises straight up from the entire area of the coal bed—as it is supposed to for effective cooking—and it carries with it the smoke produced by the burning fuel and the smoldering drippings. The volume of smoke given off varies according to the type of fuel used and the kind of food on the grill (charcoal and briquets produce little or no smoke).

For outdoor grills. It is not feasible to construct a chimney over an open-air grill, unless the grill is housed inside an outdoor fireplace and shares a common chimney. Ordinarily, the wind is relied upon to disperse the smoke and keep it away from the dining area while the food is cooking.

Of course, if the outdoor grill has a built-in hot plate that seals over the top of the firebox, that is a different story, for the plate shuts off the updraft from the fire. A short 5 to 8-foot chimney, placed at one side or the back, is necessary to carry off smoke from the fuel and to insure sound draft.

For indoor grills. A grill that is located indoors or under a shelter roof requires an efficient chimney to keep the cooking smoke from escaping into the enclosed area. The fumes may be drawn off in one of three ways: The grill may be built into a fireplace-like structure and vented with a conventional fireplace chimney; the grill may be built out from the wall like a range and vented through an overhead hood, coned to fit into a flue; or a new type of electric grill with fan immediately below can be built into a kitchen counter—the fan draws smoke and cooking odors down through

VENTILATION SYSTEM of indoor counter grill draws smoke and greasy vapors down; collects grease in a jar under the counter, then expels smoke and odors through the side of the house.

the grill and expels them through the side of the house (see above).

If a hood is used, it should be somewhat larger all around than the outside dimensions of the grill area, and it should be low enough to catch the smoke and yet not so low that it strikes the cook's head. Normally, the bottom edge of a hood is installed about 6 feet 3 inches above floor level. To insure positive ventilation that is not influenced by the vagaries of wind and weather, install an exhaust fan in the outlet. It should be capable of moving 100 cubic feet of air per square foot of hood opening.

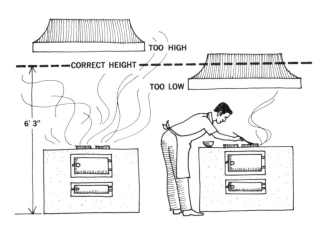

A damper may be useful in areas where wind is bothersome. It is particularly effective for indoor grills to prevent cold air from pouring down the flue when the barbecue is not in use.

Chimney flues. Ideally, the chimney flue of a barbecue grill should have a smooth inner surface to insure maximum drawing efficiency and to facilitate occasional cleaning. Clay flue tile or galvanized iron furnace conduit meet this standard most readily. Brick is satisfactory if it is evenly finished off on the inside.

Size of flue. The size of the flue you install depends on the size of the firebox and its various openings. Roughly, the cross-sectional area of the flue should not be less than 1/10 the total *open* area of the firebox.

In a fireplace-type installation, the open area is considered as the opening of the front of the fireplace. If such an opening measured 30x20 inches, or 600 square inches, the matching flue would measure 1/10 this area, or 60 square inches.

For an open-type grill, located below a hood, the flue size is related to the dimensions of the grill opening. Thus, a grill 17x30 inches, or 510 square inches, would take a flue of 51 square inches cross-section. Other openings, such as draft doors, open ash pit, etc., should be added into the total grill area.

Multiple flues. With units that have more than one flue—as in a combination indoor barbecue and fireplace—each flue should continue separately right up to the chimney top to insure good draft. This can be accomplished either with separate clay tile linings or with divisions made of galvanized metal.

Working with Concrete

Laying a concrete foundation is a respectable undertaking for any weekend mason. Those who have not worked with concrete before will discover two things: Cement is very heavy (each sack weighs about 100 pounds) and it sets up very fast once water is added. If you know the approximate shape and size of your barbecue foundation, you can order the concrete before you touch a shovel to the soil. Allow for some extra just in case the hole you dig turns out to be larger than your expectations. If you prefer, you can dig out the bed, measure it, and then order the exact amount of concrete to fill it.

You will need these tools and materials: pick, shovel, hammer, level, some old lumber, some string, and a half-pound of 10-penny nails.

Preparing the foundation bed

Preparing a bed for your barbecue foundation often turns out to be more of a task than mixing and pouring the concrete that fills it.

For a concrete slab. Lay out the boundaries of the barbecue with stakes and string. Excavate to the required depth (see page 50) and carefully level the bottom surface. If the walls of the pit hold their shape, no wooden forms need be built to hold the edge in line. But if the soil crumbles, or if you chanced to dig out the wall erratically, or if the foundation is to extend above grade, build a

retaining form of old lumber, snugly butted together. Brace it well on the outside so it can resist the pressure of the fluid concrete. Paint the inner surface of the wood with whitewash or crankcase drainings, or cover it with heavy polyethylene, so the forms can be easily removed after the concrete has set.

Build the forms up to the surface line to which you will fill. Check each side with the level; then check the level of opposite sides by placing the spirit level on a long, straight board rested on the

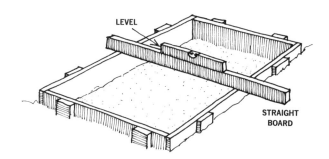

CHECK LEVEL of form with spirit level and board.

opposite walls of the form. If forms are to be built above the filling level, indicate the pouring line with a string running around the four sides. Line up the string with the level, then nail it in place.

Before pouring the concrete, soak the pit thoroughly and let it stand for a while. A dry soil will suck water from the fresh concrete and weaken it.

For a continuous footing. Dig a foundation trench in the shape of the barbecue walls. If you dig to any depth, you will undoubtedly have to prepare a trench much wider than the wall itself. Narrow the trench to the exact width by building a

USE WOODEN FORM to assure accurate outside measurement of footing; rough edge of trench is inner wall.

wooden form to support one side of the foundation wall, and use one wall of the trench to support the other.

Recommended formula

Concrete is a mixture of cement, sand, gravel, and water that is bonded together by a chemical reaction between the water and the cement. The character of the concrete is determined by the proportions used for these four ingredients. The most critical relationship in the formula is the water-cement ratio; quantities of sand and gravel may be varied slightly without affecting the strength of the mass, but the proportion of water to cement must be exactly observed.

The recommended formula for mixing a concrete barbecue foundation is:

     1 part cement
    2½ parts sand
    4 parts gravel or crushed stone

To this mixture add 5 gallons of water for each sack of cement. Sand used in concrete must be clean river sand; the seashore variety won't bond.

Gravel should range in size from ¼ to 1½ inches. The easiest way to keep track of the formula is to apply it by the shovelful. For each shovel of cement, figure about 3 quarts of water (based on an average of 6 to 7 shovelfuls of cement per sack).

Types of concrete mixes

There are several types of mix to choose from: you may buy the cement, sand, and gravel and blend them yourself; or you may get the sand and gravel already mixed, requiring only the addition of cement; or you may buy all three ingredients premixed, either wet or dry.

"Dry-Mix" concrete, which is sold under various trade names, consists of cement, sand, and gravel that are factory-blended and bagged. With the addition of water, this mix is ready for use. This is a relatively expensive way to buy the dry ingredients; but it is a convenient form to use for small or medium-sized projects, because it eliminates the drudgery of blending the ingredients in their dry state.

"Ready-Mix" concrete, also called "transit-mix," is delivered to your door wet, ready to pour. It is prepared in a giant truck with a revolving drum that mixes it while the truck is on its way to your home. Surprisingly, concrete in this form usually costs about the same as the home-made variety.

Estimating the amount required

Concrete mix, either wet or dry, is sold by cubic measure. To determine the amount you will need, compute the total number of cubic feet in your barbecue foundation and order the quantity of concrete that will fill this area. The exact amount to order will depend upon whether you are using wet or dry mix.

Dry concrete compacts when water is added to it. A cubic foot of dry mixture will occupy only about ⅔ of a cubic foot in your foundation after it has been mixed with water. You will thus have to order a greater volume of raw material than that of the area to be filled.

On the other hand, wet concrete delivered by truck should be ordered in the exact quantity needed, assuming that you can use the 27-cubic-foot minimum load. Incidentally, if *more* than 27 cubic feet is needed, the load can be made up in any quantity that you request. Have it mixed to the recommended formula (1 part cement; 2½ parts sand; 4 parts gravel).

Estimating table. Compute the cubic volume of your barbecue foundation and figure your material requirements from this table:

	Cubic Ft. in Foundation			
	5	10	20	27
Separate Ingredients				
Cement (sacks)	1	2	4	6
Sand (cubic feet)	2½	5	10	14½
Gravel (cubic feet)	4	8	16	23
Dry-Mix (sacks)	8	16	32	41
Ready-Mix (cu. yards)	0	0	0	1

In some localities, sand and gravel are sold by weight rather than by cubic foot. A cubic foot of sand or gravel weighs between 90 and 120 pounds, depending on how damp it is. Small quantities of sand are often sold by the sack. Each sack of sand (or cement) equals a cubic foot. Allow 5 per cent for wastage.

Mixing the concrete

If you plan to mix your own or to use prepared dry-mix, you will need a water pail marked off to show gallons and quarts, and two shovels (one for mixing dry materials, the other for blending wet).

Build a makeshift platform of old lumber about 4 feet square. Don't use lumber that is badly warped or full of knots, as it will let the water trickle through and weaken the concrete. An old square of plywood makes an excellent mixing surface. If you prefer to mix with a hoe, build a "boat" with 2x10's for the sides, 2x12's for the

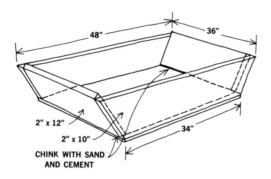

USE PLYWOOD "BOAT" for mixing concrete with hoe.

ends, and a floor of 1x6's, plywood, or galvanized metal. A boat 3 feet wide, 4 feet long will hold a 1-sack batch (see drawing).

Hand mixing. To prepare concrete from dry ingredients, heap the mixings on the board, one shovelful at a time, keeping the proportions in line with the formula, and blend the ingredients together. To save effort, learn to use the shovel with a rolling

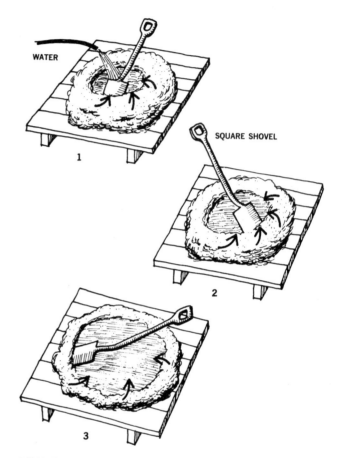

ROLL DRY CEMENT into puddle; add water if needed.

motion, turning the ingredients under with the blade. You will find this less tiring than the scoop-lift-dump method. After you have thoroughly blended the dry aggregate and cement, scoop out a hollow in the center of the heap, and fill it partly full of water. Mix in the water by working your way around the edge of the puddle with the shovel, rolling the dry mix into the water with the blade. Be careful not to break the dam, for if much water escapes, the batch will be weakened.

If you are working with the separate ingredients, first make a trial batch to test the workability of the formula. The mounds of sand and gravel that you bought are certain to contain enough moisture to require you to vary the formula slightly. To make the test batch, spread 2½ shovelfuls of sand on the mixing board and add 1 shovelful of cement. Blend together until no gray or brown streaks remain. Then, spread 4 shovelfuls of gravel over the cement-sand mixture and blend until the gravel is evenly distributed. Scoop out the center, pour in 3 quarts of water and mix it in. If the trial batch is too soupy, add a small amount of sand or gravel. If it is too stiff, cut down the quantity of sand or gravel in the next batch. Do not change the quantity of water. Dump the batch into the foundation pit and proceed with the job, mixing to the adjusted formula worked out in this batch.

If you use a prepared dry-mix, you probably won't need to try a test batch. If the mix has been manufactured and marketed under proper conditions, it should not require any adjustment in the amount of water called for in the instructions printed on the bag. Just empty 2 or 3 sacks on the mixing board, form the heap into volcano-shape, and work in the required amount of water, usually 1 gallon per bag.

Machine mixing. Old hands will tell you there is a limit to the amount of concrete that you can comfortably mix at one time on the board or in a boat. If your requirements are for a large volume of concrete, you will save time and sweat by renting a portable mixer and a wheelbarrow. The most efficient mixer for a one or two-man job is the half-bag machine. These are revolved by gasoline or electric motors or by hand. Stay away from the latter . . . it's not much fun.

Allow the mixture to tumble for 2 or 3 minutes after the water has been added, then pour into a wheelbarrow and dump into the pit.

Pouring the concrete

Pour each batch of concrete in place and tamp it down within 30 minutes, using a shovel blade or a section of 2x4. It is best to pour in all-over layers. For a two-day job, roughen the top surface of the first day's pour just before it hardens. Next day, sluice it off with a hose, and with an old broom, brush on a creamy paste of cement and water just before adding the fresh batch.

When the pit is half-filled, lay the reinforcing steel in place. Use rods, fence wire, or reinforcing mat. Tamp the concrete around and through this grid so it will be completely encased. When concrete fills to the surface line, skim it level with the edge of a long, straight board. Check the surface with the level and smooth irregularities with a flat wooden trowel known as a "float."

When the job is finished, clean out the mixer and rinse off the tools to prevent their rusting. Wet down the concrete and cover it with dirt, canvas, gunny sacks, straw, or what-have-you to slow evaporation of the water. Keep the slab damp for several days. You can begin laying brick on it two days after you finish pouring, but leave the forms in place for 10 days. Sprinkle the surface with water daily for two weeks, even after the barbecue is completed.

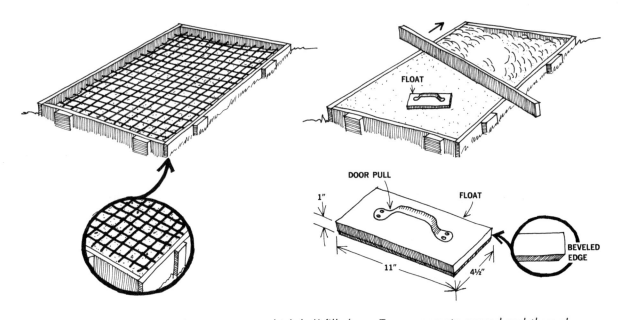

LAY REINFORCING WIRE or rods on concrete which half fills form. Tamp concrete around and through this grid. Continue filling form with concrete to surface level; skim with board; trowel with float.

Building with Brick and Mortar

Most barbecues are built of brick, and with good reason. Common brick is readily obtainable; its standard size simplifies figuring dimensions and quantities; it is inexpensive; and best of all, it is easy for an amateur to handle. It can be used throughout the entire barbecue structure, although some masons prefer to substitute firebrick in the parts that are subject to intense heat.

Your local building supply dealer probably stocks several different kinds, colors, grades, and sizes. Almost any variety that appeals to you is suitable. But try to buy brick that is well-burned, because it will take heat better than "green" brick. You can tell if a brick is hard-burned by striking it with a hammer. It should give off a clear, high-pitched sound; an under-done brick will respond with a dull thud like a block of wood. If you can't obtain hard-burned brick, you can use the softer kinds providing they are insulated from the fire with a layer of firebrick.

Used bricks, with their uneven surface and streaks of old mortar, make an attractive informal barbecue. They can often be bought in their raw state for less than new bricks; but cleaning them is a time-consuming chore, especially if the old mortar is tougher than the bricks themselves. If you buy them already cleaned, you are likely to pay more than for new brick, because of the labor involved in cleaning them up for sale.

Estimating number of bricks

The common dimensions for building brick are 8 to 8¼ inches in length, 3¾ to 3⅞ inches in width, and 2¼ to 2½ inches in depth. *These dimensions are the ones upon which the plans and estimates in this book are based.*

To estimate the number of bricks required for your barbecue, figure from your plan the number of square feet of surface in the walls and chimney. If the walls and chimney are one brick wide, multiply the total square footage by 6½. If they are double width, multiply by 13. If you intend to make the counter tops of brick, compute their total square footage and multiply by 4. (*Note:* These computations are based on the use of ½-inch mortar joint.)

Caution. You may find that bricks in your locality, or even within a single supply yard, will vary as much as a half inch from one or another of the standard dimensions. Such a variation can throw you off if you are following a plan keyed to standard sizes. A brick that is a half inch longer than standard will pick up its own width every eighth brick. Some of this excess can be reduced by narrowing the mortar joints, but even then the difference may be great enough to affect the fitting of the metal parts, such as grill, grate, and doors, or to cause the structure to overhang the edge of the foundation slab. You had better secure the exact dimensions of the bricks available from your dealer before you get too far into the project. If only over-size bricks are available, adjust the plan dimensions accordingly.

Mortar for bricklaying

Mortar is a mixture of cement, fine sand, and water with a small amount of lime or fireclay added for plasticity. Both lime and fireclay serve to make the mortar spread easily, but fireclay has the added property of being heat resistant, so it is used instead of lime in mortar that will be in contact with the flame, as in the firebox. Many brickmasons use fireclay-cement mortar throughout the entire barbecue structure. Since they have to mix it for the firebox anyway, they save the bother of preparing a different type of mortar for the rest of the unit. Fireclay-cement mortar is just as suitable as lime-cement for over-all use.

Recommended formula. For either fireclay-cement or lime-cement mortar, the ratio of sand to cement is the same:

> 1 part cement
> 4½ parts clean, fine sand

To make fireclay-cement mortar, add ½ part fireclay. For lime-cement mortar, add ½ part of hydrated lime.

If you want to avoid the labor of mixing your own dry ingredients and don't mind paying a substantial difference in price, you can buy dry-mix mortar, bagged and ready for use when you add water. Most brands of premixed mortar are made with fireclay, so they may safely be used in the firebox.

Estimating the quantity. In ordering the dry ingredients for mix-your-own mortar, use the following as a rough guide:

No. Bricks	Cement	Sand	Fireclay or Lime
250	1 sack	4½ cu. ft.	1 sack
500	2 sacks	9 cu. ft.	2 sacks
1000	4 sacks	18 cu. ft	4 sacks

A sack of cement (100 lbs.), a sack of hydrated lime or fireclay (50 lbs.), and a sack of sand (100 lbs.) equals approximately one cubic foot.

To order dry-mix mortar, figure 50 bricks to a sack.

How to mix mortar. You can use almost any flat surface for mixing mortar: a small platform made of 1x4's laid close together, an old wheelbarrow, a wooden box, or a square of plywood. Mix it in small batches so it will not dry out. Here is a reasonable amount to try, sufficient for about 50 bricks.

> 1 shovelful of cement
> 4½ shovelfuls of sand
> ½ shovelful of fireclay or lime

Mix the ingredients thoroughly in their dry state with a hoe or shovel. Scoop out a hollow, add water, and mix carefully. Continue blending and adding water until the mortar slips cleanly off the blade of the mixing tool. If a batch starts to dry out while in use, add a small amount of water and mix thoroughly. Use it up within an hour.

How to lay brick

To lay bricks, you will need a few tools. Two of them will come right out of the mason's tool bag: a sturdy, pointed trowel with a 10-inch blade, for spreading the mortar, and a broad-bladed cold chisel known as a "brick set," for cutting bricks.

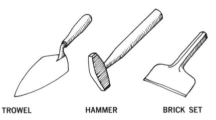

TROWEL   HAMMER   BRICK SET

Other tools will come from your workshop: a soft-headed steel hammer, a 3-foot spirit level, a carpenter's square, a length of old fishing line. You will also need a piece of straight wood 4 or 5 feet long. If you want to attempt a truly professional-looking job, you may wish to invest in additional mason's tools, such as a pointing trowel and a jointer or two.

Common bricks should be damp, but not wet, when they are laid. If they are too wet, they dilute the mortar and cause it to run, and they slip in the mortar bed. If you plan to work on your barbecue in the morning, let a very fine spray play over the brick pile for the last hour and a half of the afternoon before. For bricks you are going to lay in the afternoon, start this process in the morning about four hours before you plan to use them.

Before you start mortaring the bricks in place, experiment with lining them up dry to check on your measurements. Place a loose row of them around the foundation slab, 2 inches in from the edge. If the bricks seem to fill to your guide lines properly, with ½ inch open between each brick for the mortar joint, begin setting them with mortar.

Slice a trowel-full of mortar from the mortarboard and spread it ½ inch thick on the slab where you plan to set the brick. Roughen the mortar bed with the point of the trowel and press the brick firmly in place. Trim off excess mortar and spread it on the end of the brick facing the next

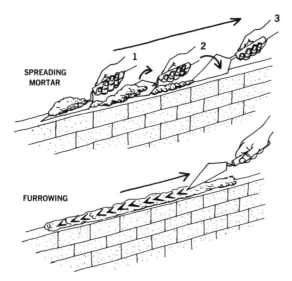

SPREADING MORTAR

FURROWING

SPREAD MORTAR ¹/₂ inch thick; furrow with trowel.

one coming up. Bricklayers usually lay about three bricks at a time; novices had better start with one.

It is best to begin with the corners. Set up a corner by laying two or three courses (or "rows") at right angles to each other, dovetailed where they meet. Check with the spirit level to make sure the courses are plumb and level; verify your right angle with the carpenter's square. When you finish a corner, go on to the next one. After you

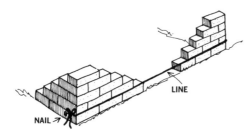

LINE

NAIL

LAY CORNER BRICKS; use guideline to fill center.

complete it, check it with the level and square, measure its height, then run a guide line between the two corners (see sketch) and brick-in the intervening space. Be sure to overlap each vertical joint with a full brick. Use the level frequently to keep the wall running true, placing it on top of the long, straight board to test levelness of the longer spans of brickwork.

If a brick slips out of place before it has set, scrape out the mortar bed, replace with fresh mortar, and then re-seat the brick.

If you have to cut a brick to make it fit, use the brick set. Place the brick on a solid, level base. Hold the blade of the set against the brick, bevel

toward the part you intend to cut off, and, tapping it lightly with a soft-headed steel hammer, cut a slight groove on one or more sides. Then place the set in the original position and give it a sharp blow with the hammer. (Be sure to wear safety goggles.)

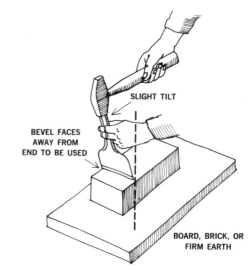

SLIGHT TILT

BEVEL FACES AWAY FROM END TO BE USED

BOARD, BRICK, OR FIRM EARTH

USE BRICK SET and soft-headed steel hammer to cut bricks.

While the mortar is still wet, trim off any loose or extruded bits and smooth off the joints. Dress the vertical ones first, then the horizontal. You may use your trowel for this operation, but you will find it much simpler to use a short piece of pipe that is slightly larger than the width of the joint—a ³/₄-inch water pipe is fine for a ¹/₂-inch joint. By drawing the pipe along the mortar joint, you can produce a smooth, concave surface. A short, rounded stick will do just as well.

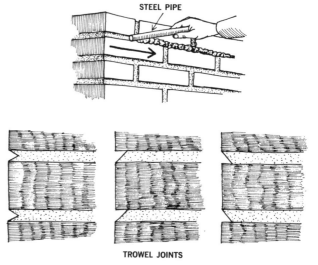

STEEL PIPE

TROWEL JOINTS

SMOOTH JOINTS with steel pipe or trowel point.

BRICK BARBECUE has grill, spit fitted into holes drilled in the sides of the firepit.

CONCRETE BLOCKS make up firebox walls, hold drop-in grill; firebox interior is lined with firebrick.

Three of the most popular trowel joints are shown here. Joints made with the trowel handle held down are preferred by many because of their water-shedding ability and because each course of bricks will throw a pleasing shadow effect that runs horizontally along the wall.

To remove mortar that has dried on brick, use a solution of 1 part muriatic acid to 9 parts water. Begin by soaking the area to be cleaned with a fine spray of water to saturate it and cut down the capillary action of the bricks. Let the water settle in, then brush the area with the acid solution (wear gloves and use a plastic bucket). Rinse thoroughly with a hose to prevent acid stains from remaining on the bricks.

Mortar will probably shrivel the skin on your fingers. There is no need for alarm; it draws natural oils out of the skin, which can be restored by rubbing in hand lotion or vaseline.

Firebrick for severe heat

Firebricks are made of a type of clay that can withstand severe temperature changes that will cause a common brick to break up; so they are customarily used to line fireboxes. They are sensitive to moisture and cold, though, and tend to disintegrate if openly exposed to severe winter weather. In areas where heavy frosts are prevalent, local practice favors substitution of hard-burned common brick for lining outdoor barbecues. It is a

good idea to check with a local building supply dealer concerning the durability of firebrick in your particular locality if you have any doubt that it might not survive in your climate.

Firebricks are larger and heavier than common bricks. Their standard dimensions are 9 by $4\frac{1}{2}$ by $2\frac{1}{2}$ inches. Installing them involves different practices from those used for common brick. Here are the principal variations:

- Never dampen firebrick before setting. Lay them bone dry.
- Butter them lightly with mortar. A $\frac{1}{16}$-inch joint is standard, but up to $\frac{1}{4}$ inch is allowable. Reason: the mortar is not as good an insulator as the brick, so it is kept to a minimum.
- Use only fireclay-cement mortar.
- For economy, lay the bricks in a wall on their edges rather than their flat sides. This method takes fewer bricks, and insulates just as well.
- To cut a firebrick, make shallow guide cuts with the brick set on *all four sides* before delivering the final severing blow.

Barbecues from concrete blocks

Concrete blocks are a satisfactory material for barbecues if they are protected from heat by firebrick or hard-burned common brick. Being larger than bricks, they lay up quickly. Use mortar that is 1 part cement, $\frac{1}{2}$ part lime or fireclay, 3 parts sand.

How to Set Stonework

A stonemason might warn you against trying to build a stone barbecue yourself, contending that rock work is an exacting craft which requires years of experience.

Compared with brickwork, stonecraft is difficult. There is more weight to handle, the uneven surfaces make plumb lines difficult to achieve, and the individual stones are hard to cut and shape. Setting heavy rocks in place is no child's game, particularly when work reaches the point where you must heft small boulders above chest height. The heavy stones squash the mortar bed, jam in wrong positions, or just refuse to fit in.

But don't be scared away if you have good reasons for making the try. You may have more rocks than plants in your garden, or a source of fieldstones may be closer than a brickyard; your site may be too primitive for bricks, or perhaps you are challenged by the stubborn quality of stone. If you follow a few simple rules and don't mind really hard labor, you should be able to do a respectable job.

Kinds of stones

Almost any kind of stone that is available in quantity may be used, although some types are more satisfactory than others. From a heat-resistant standpoint, the most suitable rocks are the tough old granites and basalts. They were fired in the earth's geologic kilns at temperatures far above any they will meet in a barbecue or fireplace, and they may thus be placed in direct contact with flames.

Their very toughness, though, makes them an obstinate material to handle. They are hard to break and chip; in fact, an amateur is likely to injure himself in attempting it. They are also slow to lay up, because they absorb so little water from the mortar that they delay its drying time.

The easiest stones to trim and face are the stratified rocks, such as limestone, shale, and sandstone. As their name implies, they are formed of *layers* of solidified soil deposit, a property that makes some of them easy to split and chip. However, they have a serious flaw: either extreme heat or cold will make them come apart at the seams. When exposed to the direct heat of a fire, they discharge hot chips; some have even been known to explode. In winter, they will absorb moisture and then split open when it turns to ice during a freezing spell. However, if you want to build your barbecue of stratified stone, you can overcome these unfortunate traits. If you trowel in your mortar solidly to prevent water from infiltrating and if you apply a good masonry sealer a few months after the job is done, your barbecue should weather a hostile winter satisfactorily. As for the explosive quality, if you shield the stone from fire with a layer of insulating brick, you needn't fear that your barbecue will ambush your guests.

Types of stonework

Stonework is divided into two broad classes: *rubble* and *ashlar*. Rubble masonry is composed of uncut stones, fitted into the structure in their natural state. Ashlar masonry is built with cut stones, laid in regular courses, like brick. Unstratified stones are often set in rubble form because they are so difficult and expensive to cut; and layered rocks are usually found in ashlar work, because they are easily dressed by the quarryman's saws and cutters.

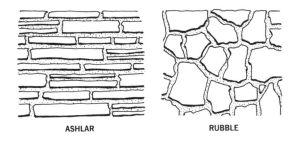

ASHLAR   RUBBLE

A barbecue can be built with either cut or uncut stones. An amateur may find ashlar easier to use than rubble, because the shaped stones can be set in place with less juggling than the rounded and irregular field stones. However, dressed stones are usually more costly.

Stonework patterns

The irregular sizes, shapes, and colors of stone give the stoneworker free range in design, and it is often because of this that the amateur comes up with a monstrosity. If properly placed, stones should produce harmonious and pleasing patterns in which there is variety but good composition. The finished structure should appear to be a unit rather than a conglomeration of rocks.

Here are some ways of insuring good, solid design:

■ The individual stones should be laid as they would lie naturally on the ground. They should rarely be placed on end or in unnatural positions.

■ Continuous wavy joints between stones should be avoided where the resulting "lightning bolt" pattern will destroy the feeling of strength and solidity inherent in all good stonework.

■ Large stones should be laid in the lower courses, small stones in the upper. This does not mean that small stones should be used *only* in the upper sections, but a larger proportion of the more solid rock is used in the base courses.

■ Stones of the same size or shape should not be set side by side. Avoid the "peanut brittle" effect by setting in a long, narrow stone or one that is much larger than the adjacent rocks.

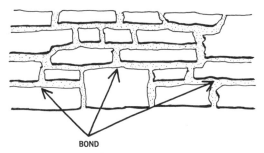

BOND

OVERLAP JOINTS with large stones for bonding.

■ A strong wall requires "bonding"—the overlapping of two small stones by one long one.

Quantity of stone required

Estimates of the amount of stone required for masonry work are usually figured in tons. The area that a ton will occupy depends, of course, on the type of stone used. For example, a ton of fieldstone will fill from 25 to 40 *cubic* feet of wall; while a ton of dressed flagstone, laid as veneer, will cover 55 *square* feet. In some localities, stone is sold by the cubic yard (27 cu. ft.), which will occupy slightly more than the same volume of wall. Your dealer is accustomed to figuring these quantities. If you provide him with the total cubic wall area in your barbecue, he will compute the amount of rock needed.

When selecting stones, choose a variety of sizes, keeping in mind the scale of the work. A good rule to remember is that the face area of the larger stones laid should not be more than 5 or 6 times the face area of the smallest stones. Large stones, of course, can sometimes be broken to size while the work is progressing. If you plan to use cut stone, order specific thicknesses and designate the upper and lower limits of length. Here, again, the longer slabs may be broken on the job.

Mortar for stonework

Stonework requires a relatively large quantity of mortar, because of the irregular size of the mortar joints and the numerous voids that have to be filled in. A structure built of fieldstone or river rock, for instance, may contain as much as one-third mortar.

Estimating the amount needed in a barbecue is largely inspired guesswork. One fairly sure way of working out the problem is to lay up a small section of the barbecue wall, figure the amount of mortar used, then compute the quantity needed for the rest of the unit and order accordingly. However, a surer way than this is to pass the whole problem over to your dealer, who can be relied upon to figure it out correctly.

Recommended formula. The formula recommended for rock mortar is richer than for brick:

> 1 part cement
> 3 parts clean sand
> ½ part fireclay

Do not use hydrated lime in place of fireclay because it is likely to discolor the stones.

Mixing mortar: See instructions on mortar mixing on page 59.

How to set stone

The tools required for cutting stones are the same as for laying brick: a heavy hammer, a mason's trowel and chisel, spirit level, a hoe, and a hank of old fishing line or mason's twine. If you plan to break rock, you will need a sledge hammer. An old broom, with the bristles cropped, will make a handy brush for cleaning excess mortar off the face of the wall. You will also need a platform or box for mixing mortar.

- Have plenty of rock handy. If you have a choice of sizes and shapes, you will not be inclined to force the job. Place the stones where you can reach them as you work. To keep your pattern interesting and insure good bonding, try several rocks in a section of the wall before mortaring.

- All stones should be cleaned thoroughly. Remove all dirt and lichen from surfaces to be mortared. Do not brush with an iron bristle-brush as this may produce latent rust stains. If you clean the stones with water, let them dry before mortaring.

- String guide lines and keep the face of the

USE STAKES AND STRING as guide for edge, height.

structure flush by selecting rocks and setting them so they do not jut beyond the face of the wall.

- Be sure the joints are properly bonded by overlapping the vertical joints at every course. Put in headers—stones set with their long dimensions at right angles to the face of the wall—to strengthen the wall transversely.

- Use enough mortar to fill *completely* all the joints. Make the joints as thin as possible. Chink, with small chips of stone, all empty spaces between rocks in the interior of the wall, and fill with mortar.

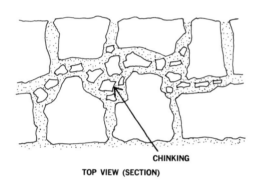

CHINKING

TOP VIEW (SECTION)

- If you have to shift a stone that is already set in mortar, lift it clear of the mortar bed, scrape off all mortar, and replace with a fresh layer.

- After you have laid one section, rake out the joints on the facing before the mortar sets. Use a stick with a dull point. The rake should be ½ to ¾ of an inch—the deeper the rake, the better the

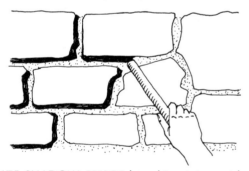

CREATE SHADOW EFFECT by raking joints with stick.

shadow effect. Thoroughly brush off all excess mortar with an old broom before it has set too firmly.

How to set stone veneer

Another way of laying up a rock barbecue wall is to set a veneer of stone over a core of hard-burned brick. This type of construction, by shielding the

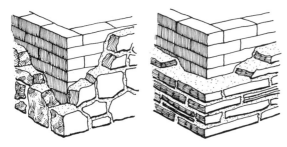

SHIELD STONE VENEER with layer of firebrick.

stone from fire, permits the use of colorful varieties of stratified stone that would otherwise be unsafe to install.

As a rule, cut stone is preferred for veneer because its squared surfaces are easily aligned with the flat planes of brick. Uncut stones may also be used, but they require more skill in setting because the small sizes needed for shallow veneer work may produce an unpleasant knobby texture unless placed with a careful eye.

Easiest type of veneer to apply is dressed sandstone, obtainable from most building supply dealers in strips 3 or 4 inches wide, 1½ inches high, and from 6 to 24 inches in length. Colors range from brick red, through buff, to yellow. It is laid like brick and is readily cut with a brick set. One important difference from brick: it must be mortared dry.

Here are some pointers on laying veneer:

▪ Lay the brick inner core first, then build the veneer around it. If you prefer, you can lay core and veneer simultaneously, but you will find it easier to keep the structure level and plumb if you build the core first.

▪ Mortar the veneer solidly to the core.

▪ For a tall structure, such as a chimney, add reinforcement in the mortar joint between the core and veneer. Use ³/₈-inch rod, set vertically on 24-inch centers, and tie in with stirrup ties.

▪ Keep mortar smears off stone by wiping it off with a wet rag as you go. If some mortar stains do appear when the work is dry, remove them with an alkali soap solution (2 bars to 1 gal. water). Apply this solution to *wet* stone, scrub, and rinse *thoroughly*. Remove soap stains with vinegar. Do not use muriatic acid on limestone or sandstone.

▪ To seal a porous rock against moisture, give the stone about six months to evaporate the water in the mortar, then brush on a good quality masonry sealer. Check the surface in four or five years. If the crust of the stone is sloughing off, apply another coat of sealer.

RUBBLE MASONRY BARBECUE, built indoors, is equipped with an easy-to-install slide-in grill.

BARBECUE-FIREPLACE combination is constructed from ashlar cut stones, laid in regular courses.

Using Your Barbecue

When construction of your barbecue unit is complete and the last smear of mortar has been removed—or when a shiny new portable unit stands ready for use—you are ready to begin barbecuing. Along with selecting the accessories that will add to the fun and convenience of cooking, it is also important to know the basic maintenance requirements necessary for a longer barbecue life.

You will find complete information on "firemanship" and other cooking techniques along with scores of barbecue recipes in the *Sunset Barbecue Cook Book*.

Barbecue accessories

A few simple barbecue accessories add greatly to the convenience and pleasure of cooking and eating outdoors. Here are some suggestions:

Cooking accessories. A long-handled roasting fork, a pair of cooking tongs (for turning meat, lifting baked potatoes and corn on the cob), a long-handled spoon, and a spatula are the handiest tools for working around the hot grill. For controlling the fire, you need a poker, preferably one with a bent tip for shoving coals around. Two types of knives complete the outdoor kit: a heavy butcher's knife, and a husky parer.

Saucepans and casseroles can probably be borrowed from your regular kitchen supply, although you may prefer to assemble a duplicate set for outdoor use. A large iron skillet with sloping sides, measuring 24 inches or more across, is convenient and particularly useful if your grill is not equipped with a flat plate.

Personal accessories. This classification includes a pair of canvas gloves for handling charcoal, a pair of asbestos gloves for preventing scorched fingers, and cover-all aprons. Ideal regalia for a barbecue chef is a full-length bib or butcher's apron, which is heavy and of extra width. Supplement this with a chef's folded waist apron for extra protection and for hand wiping.

Long live your barbecue

A deserving barbecue, either built-in or portable, will give many years' service if it is protected from its natural enemies—moisture, rust, and fire. Here are some suggestions for maintenance:

- Break in a masonry barbecue carefully. Do not build a fire in it for two weeks after completion. Then cure it slowly with a small fire, kept burning for four or five hours.

- Protect a masonry unit from winter weather by covering the opening of the firebox and the top of the chimney. During the rainy season, brick and stone will soak up water which will take weeks to evaporate in the spring. A water-logged barbecue

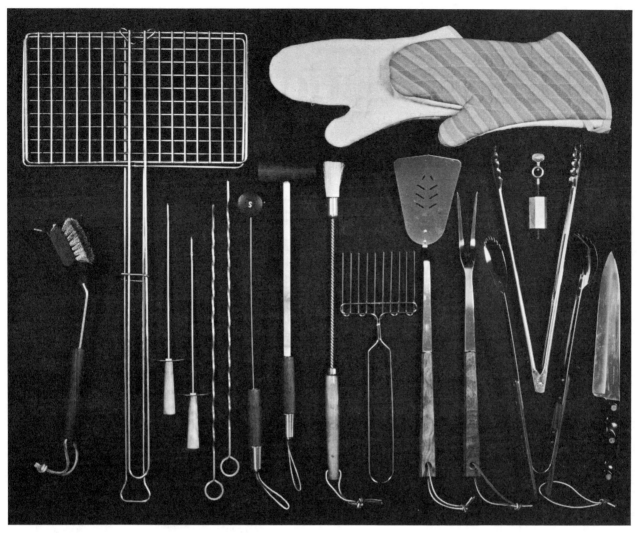

USEFUL BARBECUE ACCESSORIES include (left to right): wire brush with scraper, hinged wire broiler, skewers, salt and pepper shakers, basting brush, turning fork, tongs, and balance weight for spit.

can be injured by either a freeze or a premature barbecue fire. In one case ice does the damage; in the other, steam. Portable units should be stored under cover during rainy weather.

▪ After a severe winter, treat an unprotected barbecue like a new one, and break it in carefully with the first spring fire.

▪ Never put out the fire in a masonry barbecue with water. The sudden change in temperature is likely to crack the firebox.

▪ Keep the grill from rusting by putting it away dirty after each barbecue meal. The cooking grease will preserve it. Burn off the grease before you use it the next time, and wipe it clean with wadded newspaper or gunny sacking.

▪ Protect metal fixtures from rust by removing all detachable parts for winter storage. Clean off

specks of rust with steel wool, touch up with paint and oil, wrap in newspapers, and store in a dry place. Paint and oil built-in metalwork.

▪ Prolong the life of the grill and grate by not exposing them to fire any longer than you have to. Fire gradually destroys iron; ashes in the presence of water eat through metal. Keep the ashes cleaned out, and leave the grill off when not in use.

▪ Protect a portable metal barbecue by laying foil on the base of the unit and spreading pea gravel across it. This insulates the metal against the heat from the coals.

▪ Do not put heavy kettles on an over-heated grill. The weight will make the weakened metal sag.

▪ Keep the barbecue firebox fresh and odorless by not burning rubbish in it.

Construction Plans

The different plans in this section represent barbecue units that have actually been built. But you don't have to follow them "brick by brick." Half the fun is calling your ingenuity into play. Shift a detail or two; add a feature here; eliminate one there; so that when you're through, it's not "just another barbecue," but your own creation.

Except for the plans shown, detailed dimensional drawings for the many barbecues and out-door fireplaces shown throughout the book are not available.

Caution. Bricks vary in size, not only between locales but also within a single yard. Before starting, measure the bricks you have purchased, as well as the grates, grills and doors, and modify the plans, if necessary, to suit your materials. Plan measurements are figured for ½-inch mortar joint.

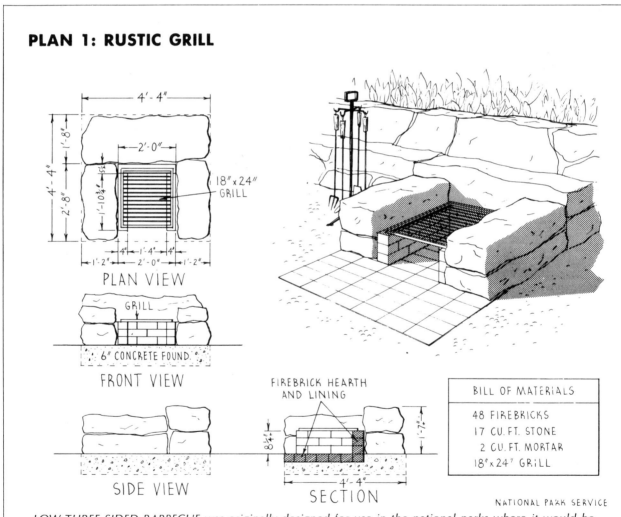

PLAN 1: RUSTIC GRILL

PLAN VIEW

FRONT VIEW

SIDE VIEW

SECTION

FIREBRICK HEARTH AND LINING

BILL OF MATERIALS
48 FIREBRICKS
17 CU. FT. STONE
2 CU. FT. MORTAR
18" x 24" GRILL

NATIONAL PARK SERVICE

LOW THREE-SIDED BARBECUE was originally designed for use in the national parks where it would be inconspicuous in a woodland setting. If desired, smaller rocks or brick may be used.

PLAN 2: GRILL AND COUNTER

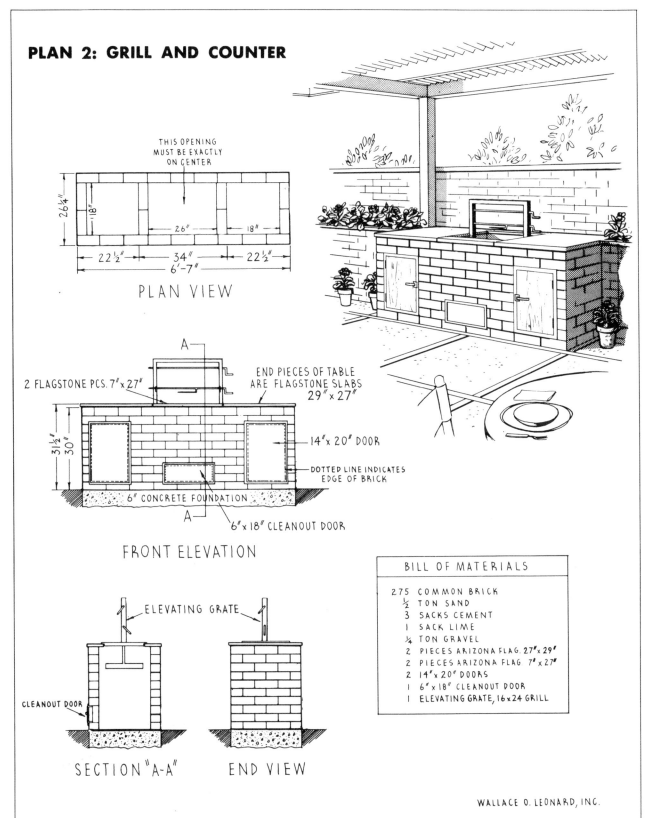

THIS OPENING
MUST BE EXACTLY
ON CENTER

26¼" 18"

26" 18"

22½" 34" 22½"

6'-7"

PLAN VIEW

A

2 FLAGSTONE PCS. 7" x 27"

END PIECES OF TABLE
ARE FLAGSTONE SLABS
29" x 27"

31½" 30"

14" x 20" DOOR

DOTTED LINE INDICATES
EDGE OF BRICK

6" CONCRETE FOUNDATION

6" x 18" CLEANOUT DOOR

A

FRONT ELEVATION

ELEVATING GRATE

CLEANOUT DOOR

SECTION "A-A"   END VIEW

BILL OF MATERIALS

275 COMMON BRICK
½ TON SAND
3 SACKS CEMENT
1 SACK LIME
¼ TON GRAVEL
2 PIECES ARIZONA FLAG. 27" x 29"
2 PIECES ARIZONA FLAG. 7" x 27"
2 14" x 20" DOORS
1 6" x 18" CLEANOUT DOOR
1 ELEVATING GRATE, 16 x 24 GRILL

WALLACE O. LEONARD, INC.

GRILL-IN-COUNTER is suitable for various installations. It can be built into a wall, constructed freestanding, or paired with matching counter as the wing of corner barbecue. Grill needn't be in center.

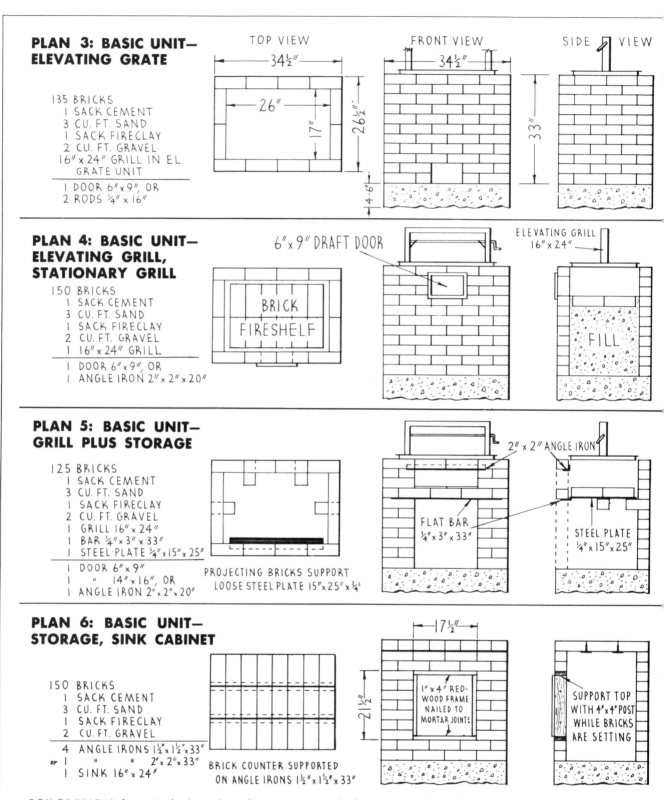

PLAN 3: BASIC UNIT—ELEVATING GRATE

TOP VIEW FRONT VIEW SIDE VIEW

135 BRICKS
1 SACK CEMENT
3 CU. FT. SAND
1 SACK FIRECLAY
2 CU. FT. GRAVEL
16" x 24" GRILL IN EL. GRATE UNIT

1 DOOR 6"x9", OR
2 RODS ¼" x 16"

PLAN 4: BASIC UNIT—ELEVATING GRILL, STATIONARY GRILL

150 BRICKS
1 SACK CEMENT
3 CU. FT. SAND
1 SACK FIRECLAY
2 CU. FT. GRAVEL
1 16" x 24" GRILL

1 DOOR 6"x9", OR
1 ANGLE IRON 2"x 2"x 20"

6"x 9" DRAFT DOOR

BRICK FIRESHELF

ELEVATING GRILL 16" x 24"

FILL

PLAN 5: BASIC UNIT—GRILL PLUS STORAGE

125 BRICKS
1 SACK CEMENT
3 CU. FT. SAND
1 SACK FIRECLAY
2 CU. FT. GRAVEL
1 GRILL 16" x 24"
1 BAR ¼" x 3" x 33"
1 STEEL PLATE ¼"x15"x 25"

1 DOOR 6"x 9"
1   "   14"x 16", OR
1 ANGLE IRON 2"x 2"x 20"

PROJECTING BRICKS SUPPORT
LOOSE STEEL PLATE 15"x25"x ¼"

2" x 2" ANGLE IRON

FLAT BAR ¼"x 3"x 33"

STEEL PLATE ¼"x15"x 25"

PLAN 6: BASIC UNIT—STORAGE, SINK CABINET

150 BRICKS
1 SACK CEMENT
3 CU. FT. SAND
1 SACK FIRECLAY
2 CU. FT. GRAVEL
4 ANGLE IRONS 1½"x 1½"x 33"
or 1   "   "   2"x 2"x 33"
1 SINK 16"x 24"

BRICK COUNTER SUPPORTED
ON ANGLE IRONS 1½"x 1½"x 33"

17½"

21½"

1" x 4" RED-WOOD FRAME NAILED TO MORTAR JOINTS

SUPPORT TOP WITH 4"x 4" POST WHILE BRICKS ARE SETTING

BOX OF BRICKS shown in the four plans above comprises the basic unit of the barbecue family. PLANS 3-5 show various ways of building a counter-height grill unit, adapted to different kinds of barbecue equipment; PLAN 6 shows how same masonry box is used for storage or sink cabinet. The basic grill may be combined with several of the plans on the following pages. PLAN 3 shows how to build a shelf for an

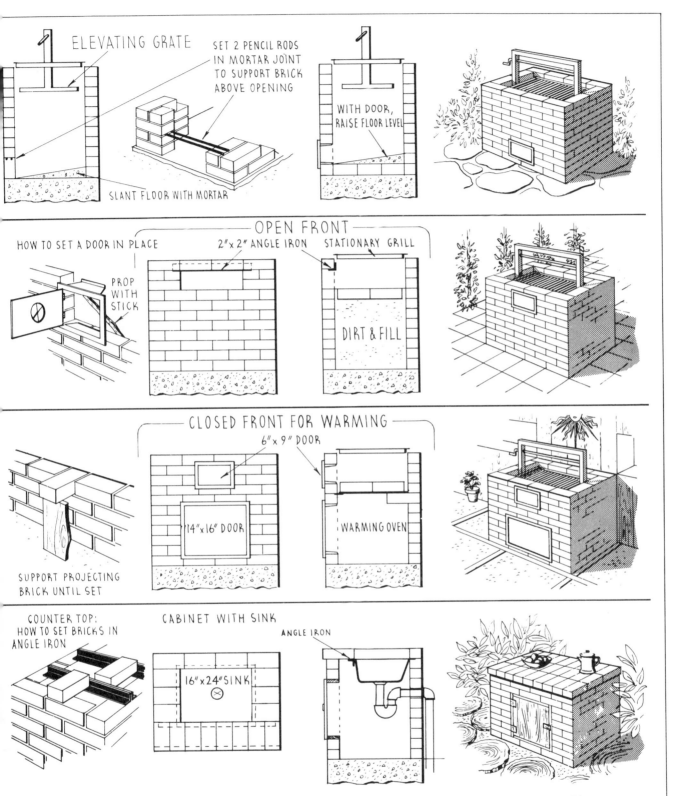

ELEVATING GRATE

SET 2 PENCIL RODS IN MORTAR JOINT TO SUPPORT BRICK ABOVE OPENING

WITH DOOR, RAISE FLOOR LEVEL

SLANT FLOOR WITH MORTAR

OPEN FRONT

HOW TO SET A DOOR IN PLACE

2" x 2" ANGLE IRON

STATIONARY GRILL

PROP WITH STICK

DIRT & FILL

CLOSED FRONT FOR WARMING

6" x 9" DOOR

SUPPORT PROJECTING BRICK UNTIL SET

14" x 16" DOOR

WARMING OVEN

COUNTER TOP: HOW TO SET BRICKS IN ANGLE IRON

CABINET WITH SINK

ANGLE IRON

16" x 24" SINK

elevating grate; note that no fireshelf is provided, for it is included in the elevating grate assembly. PLAN 4 is for an elevating or stationary grill installation. Fireshelf is not part of the fixture, so it must be built in; this has been done by resting bricks on dirt fill. PLAN 5 shows how to use space below grill. Steel fireshelf is set in loose. PLAN 6 shows storage or sink cabinet. Set counter carefully to prevent seepage.

PLAN 7: GRILL AND HOT PLATE

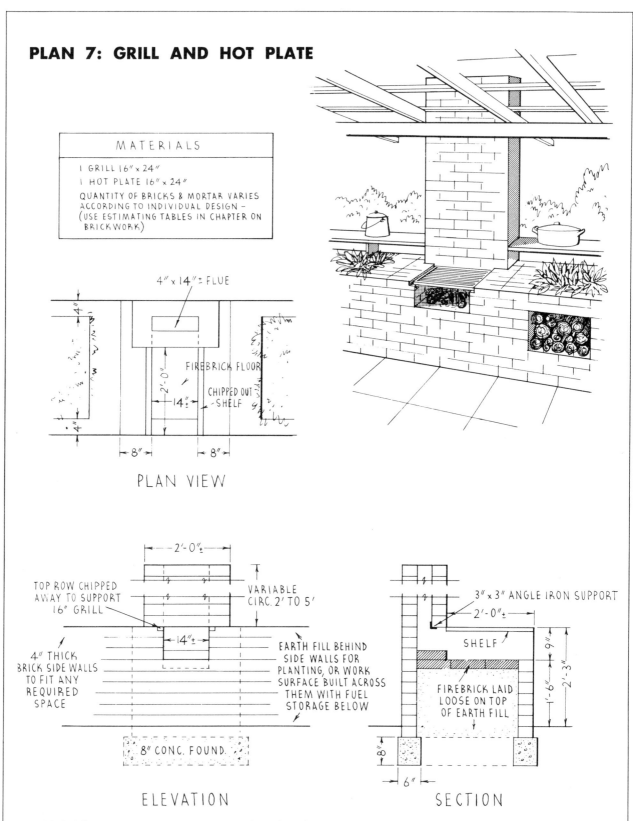

MATERIALS

1 GRILL 16" x 24"
1 HOT PLATE 16" x 24"
QUANTITY OF BRICKS & MORTAR VARIES
ACCORDING TO INDIVIDUAL DESIGN –
(USE ESTIMATING TABLES IN CHAPTER ON
BRICKWORK)

4" x 14"± FLUE

FIREBRICK FLOOR

CHIPPED OUT SHELF

2'-0"

14"±

8"   8"

PLAN VIEW

2'-0"±

TOP ROW CHIPPED AWAY TO SUPPORT 16" GRILL

VARIABLE CIRC. 2' TO 5'

14"±

4" THICK BRICK SIDE WALLS TO FIT ANY REQUIRED SPACE

EARTH FILL BEHIND SIDE WALLS FOR PLANTING, OR WORK SURFACE BUILT ACROSS THEM WITH FUEL STORAGE BELOW

8" CONC. FOUND.

ELEVATION

3" x 3" ANGLE IRON SUPPORT

2'-0"±

SHELF

9"

2'-3"

1'-6"

FIREBRICK LAID LOOSE ON TOP OF EARTH FILL

8"

6"

SECTION

BASIC COUNTER-HEIGHT GRILL is combined with an all-over hot plate for griddle cooking. Chimney provides draft when hot plate is set over firebox. The height of the chimney is optional.

PLAN 8: CONCRETE BLOCK BARBECUE

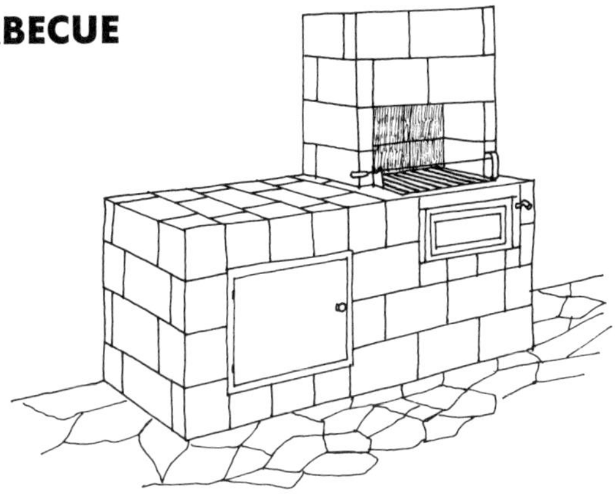

BILL OF MATERIALS

48 CONCRETE BLOCKS 4x8x16
16 CONCRETE BLOCKS 8x8x16
18 CONCRETE HALF BLOCKS 4x8x8
12 CONCRETE HALF BLOCKS 8x8x8
4 CONCRETE HALF BLOCKS 4x6x8
8 CONCRETE HALF BLOCKS 4x4x8
2 SACKS REGULAR CEMENT
1 SACK MASONRY CEMENT
½ YARD SAND
¼ YARD SAND
¼ YARD GRAVEL
1 BARBECUE UNIT
1 STEEL STORAGE DOOR
1 ELECTRIC SPIT
1 ANGLE BAR 3 x 3 x 3/16, 33"
5 REINFORCING RODS 3/8", 33" LONG
5 REINFORCING RODS 3/8", 44" LONG
12 COMMON BRICKS

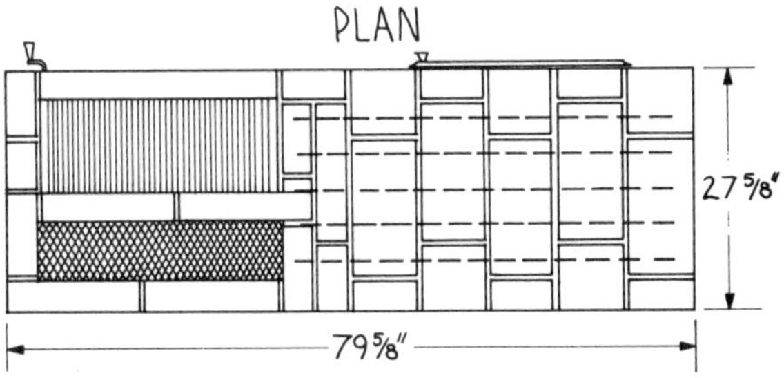

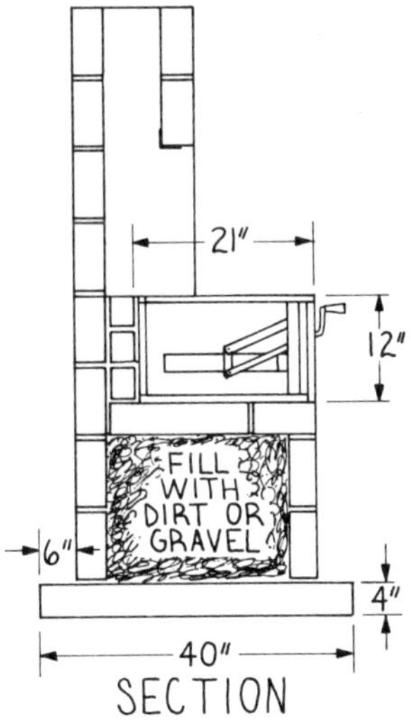

PLAN

27 5/8"

79 5/8"

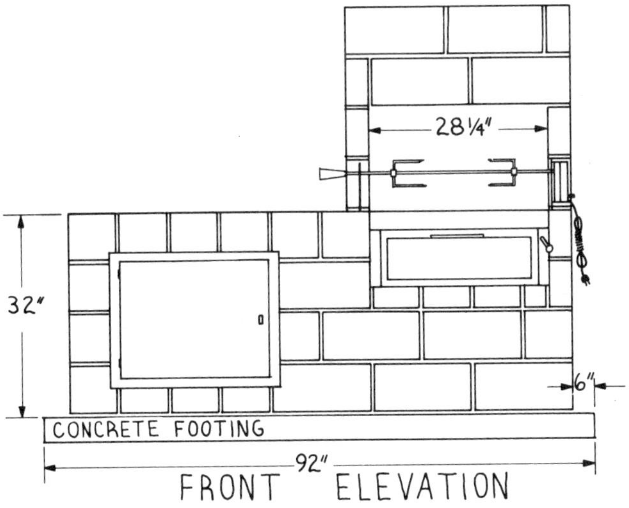

28 1/4"

32"

6"

CONCRETE FOOTING

FRONT ELEVATION

92"

21"

12"

FILL WITH DIRT OR GRAVEL

6"

4"

40"

SECTION

SUPERIOR FIREPLACE COMPANY

METAL FIXTURES, such as elevating grate assembly and metal storage door, complete this concrete block barbecue. Area under firebox is fill, and short chimney provides draft to fire.

PLAN 9: BARBECUE-FIREWALL

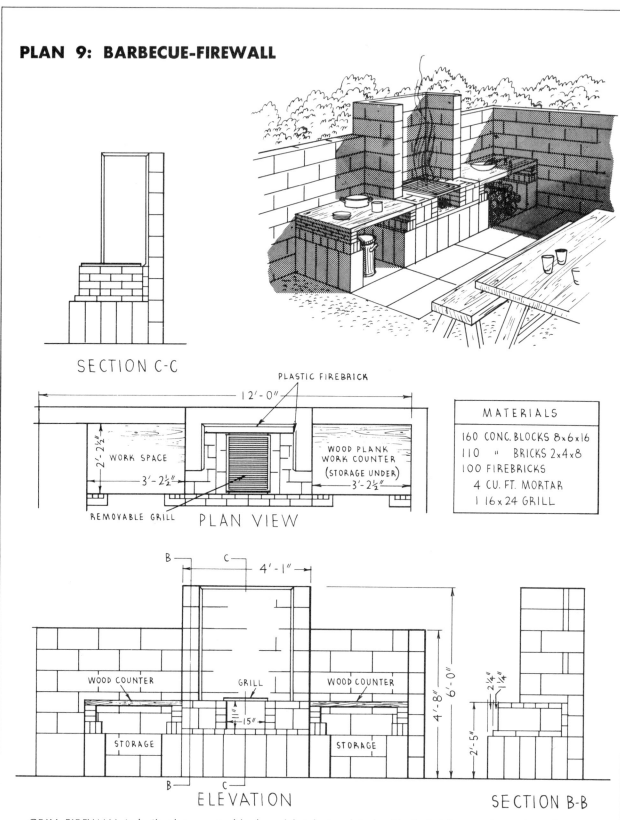

SECTION C-C

PLASTIC FIREBRICK

12'-0"

2'-2½" WORK SPACE

3'-2½"

WORD PLANK
WORK COUNTER
(STORAGE UNDER)

3'-2½"

REMOVABLE GRILL

PLAN VIEW

MATERIALS

160 CONC. BLOCKS 8x6x16
110   "   BRICKS 2x4x8
100 FIREBRICKS
  4 CU. FT. MORTAR
  1 16x24 GRILL

B   C

4'-1"

WOOD COUNTER

GRILL

WOOD COUNTER

6'-0"

4'-8"

2¼"
1¼"

15"

STORAGE

STORAGE

2'-5"

B   C

ELEVATION

SECTION B-B

GRILL-FIREWALL is built of concrete block and brick, insulated with firebrick at points where heat is greatest. Check local fire regulations before tackling this one, as there may be restrictions.

PLAN 10: BARBECUE WITH CHIMNEY

```
              MATERIALS

    88 CU. FT. STONE
    16 CU. FT. MORTAR
     1 GRILL 18 x 24
     1 GRATE 18 x 24, OR
     2 GRATES 12 x 18
```

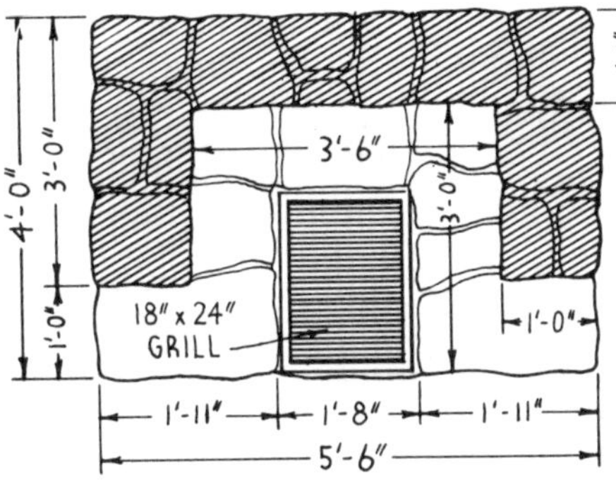

PLAN VIEW

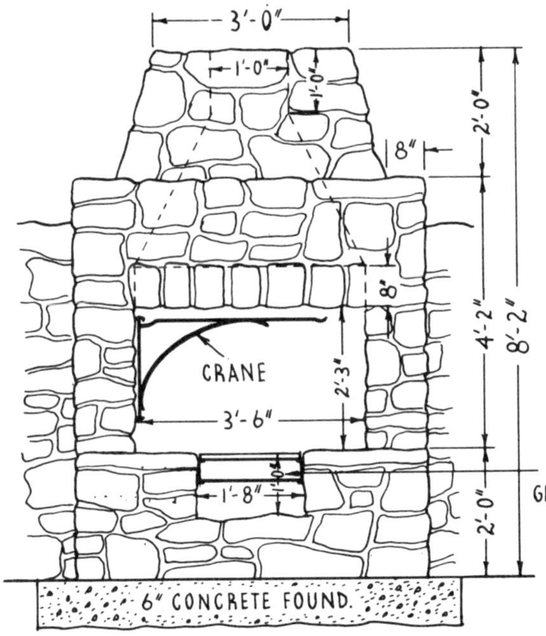

3'-6"
3'-0"
4'-0"
1'-0"
1'-0"
18" x 24" GRILL
1'-0"
1'-11" 1'-8" 1'-11"
5'-6"

ELEVATION VIEW

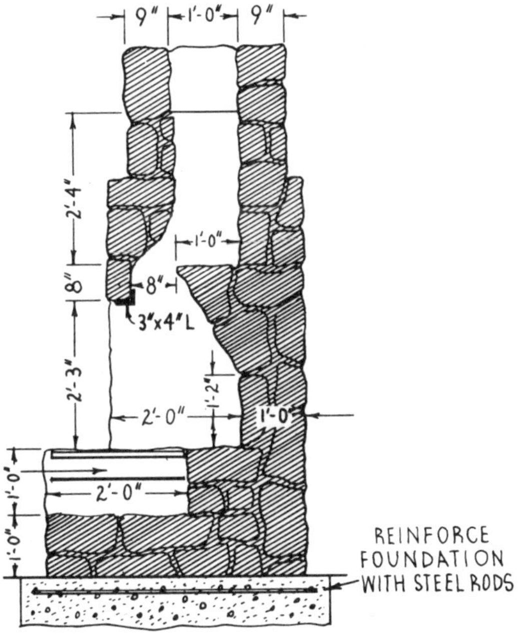

3'-0"
1'-0"
2'-0"
8"
8'
4'-2"
8'-2"
CRANE
2'-3"
3'-6"
1'-8"
2-LEVEL GRATE SLIDE
2'-0"
6" CONCRETE FOUND.

CROSS SECTION

9" 1'-0" 9"
2'-4"
8"
1'-0"
8"
3"x4" L
2'-3"
1'-2"
2'-0"
1'-0"
2'-0"
1'-0"
REINFORCE FOUNDATION WITH STEEL RODS

THE DONLEY BROS. CO.

STONE BARBECUE has chimney to carry off smoke. Wood fire is built on top of grates; when wood has burned down to coals, grates are slid out, dumping coals into recess. Grill is then set in place.

PLAN 11: SIMPLE BRICK BARBECUE

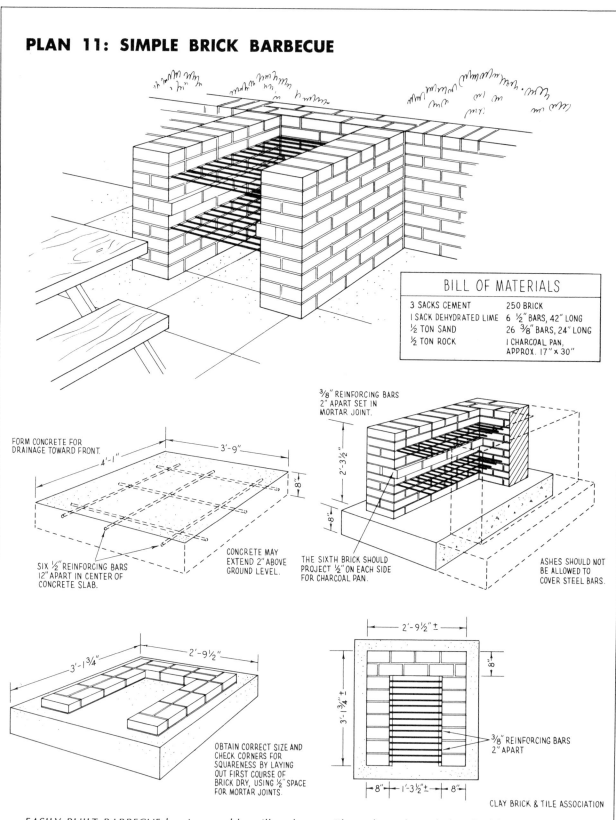

BILL OF MATERIALS

3 SACKS CEMENT	250 BRICK
1 SACK DEHYDRATED LIME	6 ½" BARS, 42" LONG
½ TON SAND	26 ⅜" BARS, 24" LONG
½ TON ROCK	1 CHARCOAL PAN, APPROX. 17" x 30"

FORM CONCRETE FOR DRAINAGE TOWARD FRONT.

4'-1"

3'-9"

8"

SIX ½" REINFORCING BARS 12" APART IN CENTER OF CONCRETE SLAB.

CONCRETE MAY EXTEND 2" ABOVE GROUND LEVEL.

⅜" REINFORCING BARS 2" APART SET IN MORTAR JOINT.

2'-3½"

8"

THE SIXTH BRICK SHOULD PROJECT ½" ON EACH SIDE FOR CHARCOAL PAN.

ASHES SHOULD NOT BE ALLOWED TO COVER STEEL BARS.

3'-1¾"

2'-9½"

OBTAIN CORRECT SIZE AND CHECK CORNERS FOR SQUARENESS BY LAYING OUT FIRST COURSE OF BRICK DRY, USING ½" SPACE FOR MORTAR JOINTS.

2'-9½" ±

8"

3'-3¾" ±

⅜" REINFORCING BARS 2" APART

8"   1'-3½"±   8"

CLAY BRICK & TILE ASSOCIATION

EASILY BUILT BARBECUE has immovable grill and grate. The only tool needed to build it is a masons trowel. There is no need for firebrick; standard building brick can be used for entire barbecue.

PLAN 12: CHINESE OVEN

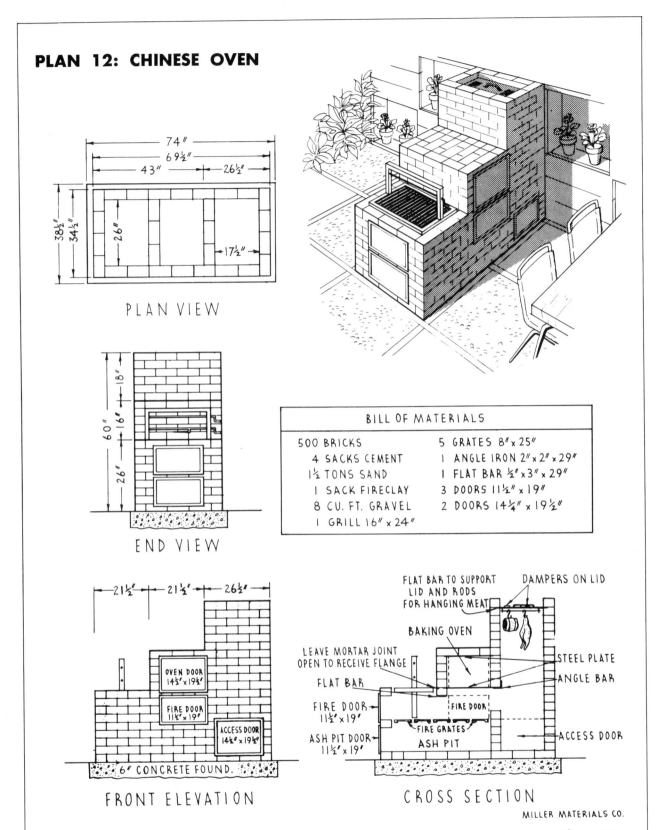

PLAN VIEW

74"
69½"
43" 26½"
38½"
34½"
26"
17½"

END VIEW

60"
18"
16"
26"

BILL OF MATERIALS

500 BRICKS
4 SACKS CEMENT
1½ TONS SAND
1 SACK FIRECLAY
8 CU. FT. GRAVEL
1 GRILL 16" x 24"

5 GRATES 8" x 25"
1 ANGLE IRON 2" x 2" x 29"
1 FLAT BAR ½" x 3" x 29"
3 DOORS 11½" x 19"
2 DOORS 14¼" x 19½"

FRONT ELEVATION

21½" 21½" 26½"

OVEN DOOR 14½" x 19½"
FIRE DOOR 11½" x 19"
ACCESS DOOR 14½" x 19½"

6" CONCRETE FOUND.

CROSS SECTION

FLAT BAR TO SUPPORT LID AND RODS FOR HANGING MEAT
DAMPERS ON LID
BAKING OVEN
LEAVE MORTAR JOINT OPEN TO RECEIVE FLANGE
STEEL PLATE
FLAT BAR
ANGLE BAR
FIRE DOOR 11½" x 19"
FIRE DOOR
FIRE GRATES
ASH PIT DOOR 11½" x 19"
ACCESS DOOR
ASH PIT

MILLER MATERIALS CO.

SMOKE OVEN part of this combination should be built of firebrick if it is to be used often (or at least very hard common brick). If firebrick is used, its larger size must be considered in plans.

PLAN 13: FLAT-TOP GRILL (BRICK)

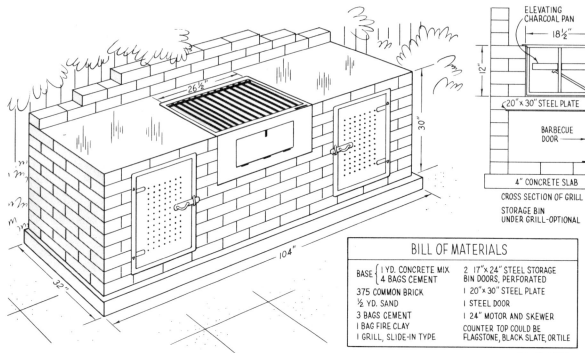

ELEVATING
CHARCOAL PAN

18½"

12"

20"x 30" STEEL PLATE

BARBECUE
DOOR

4" CONCRETE SLAB

CROSS SECTION OF GRILL

STORAGE BIN
UNDER GRILL-OPTIONAL

BILL OF MATERIALS	
BASE { 1 YD. CONCRETE MIX, 4 BAGS CEMENT	2 17"x 24" STEEL STORAGE BIN DOORS, PERFORATED
375 COMMON BRICK	1 20"x 30" STEEL PLATE
½ YD. SAND	1 STEEL DOOR
3 BAGS CEMENT	1 24" MOTOR AND SKEWER
1 BAG FIRE CLAY	COUNTER TOP COULD BE
1 GRILL, SLIDE-IN TYPE	FLAGSTONE, BLACK SLATE, OR TILE

MILLER MATERIALS CO.

PLAN 14: FLAT-TOP GRILL (STONE)

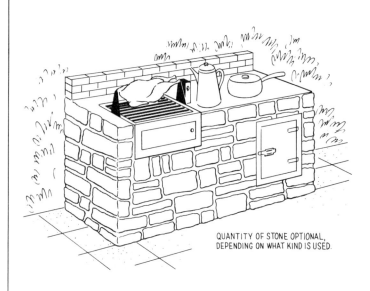

QUANTITY OF STONE OPTIONAL,
DEPENDING ON WHAT KIND IS USED.

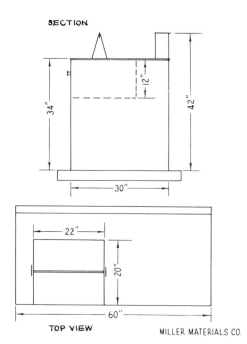

SECTION

34"

12"

42"

30"

22"

20"

60"

TOP VIEW

MILLER MATERIALS CO.

CHIMNEYLESS FLAT-TOPS are economical, easy-to-build. Perforated metal doors in brick barbecue keep storage area ventilated and dry. Both examples use slide-in grills, but are easily adapted to drop-in type.

PLAN 15: DEEP-PIT BARBECUE

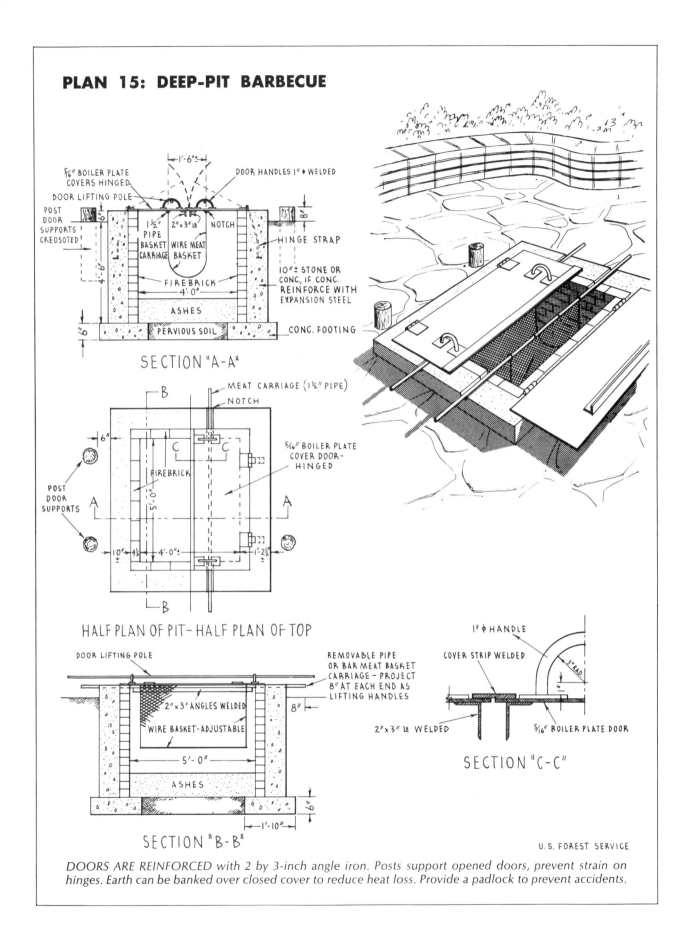

SECTION "A-A"

5/16" BOILER PLATE COVERS HINGED
DOOR LIFTING POLE
POST DOOR SUPPORTS CREOSOTED
1½" PIPE BASKET CARRIAGE
2"x3" L
WIRE MEAT BASKET
NOTCH
FIREBRICK
4'-0"
ASHES
PERVIOUS SOIL
DOOR HANDLES 1" ⌀ WELDED
HINGE STRAP
10"± STONE OR CONC., IF CONC. REINFORCE WITH EXPANSION STEEL
CONC. FOOTING

HALF PLAN OF PIT—HALF PLAN OF TOP

MEAT CARRIAGE (1½" PIPE)
NOTCH
5/16" BOILER PLATE COVER DOOR-HINGED
FIREBRICK
POST DOOR SUPPORTS
5'-0"
10"± 1½" 4'-0"± 1'-2½"

SECTION "B-B"

DOOR LIFTING POLE
REMOVABLE PIPE OR BAR MEAT BASKET CARRIAGE—PROJECT 8" AT EACH END AS LIFTING HANDLES
2"x3" ANGLES WELDED
WIRE BASKET-ADJUSTABLE
8"
5'-0"
ASHES
6"
1'-10"

SECTION "C-C"

1" ⌀ HANDLE
COVER STRIP WELDED
3" RAD.
2"x3" L WELDED
5/16" BOILER PLATE DOOR

U.S. FOREST SERVICE

DOORS ARE REINFORCED with 2 by 3-inch angle iron. Posts support opened doors, prevent strain on hinges. Earth can be banked over closed cover to reduce heat loss. Provide a padlock to prevent accidents.

Sunset
Proof-of-Purchase
ISBN 0-376-01042-8

PHOTOGRAPHERS

B. J. Allen: page 12 (left). **Jerry A. Anson:** page 38 (left). **William Aplin:** page 17 (bottom). **Aplin-Dudley Studios:** page 34 (bottom). **Morley Baer:** page 61 (right). **Ernest Braun:** pages 24 (top), 25 (top), 30 (top), 32 (left), 32-33. **Tony Caldwell:** pages 21 (top), 31 (bottom), 37 (right). **Char-Broil:** page 11. **Clyde Childress:** page 40. **Glenn M. Christiansen:** pages 16 (bottom left, right), 20, 24 (bottom). **Kenneth Cooperrider:** page 42. **Robert Cox:** pages 14-15 (top), 26 (left), 28-29 (top), 38-39. **Dearborn-Massar:** pages 36-37 (top). **Richard Fish:** page 30 (bottom). **Frank L. Gaynor:** page 15 (bottom left). **D. J. Higgins:** page 35 (bottom). **Larry Kenney:** page 19 (top left). **Lee Klein:** pages 13 (right), 15 (right), 18, 19 (top right, bottom), 22 (left), 26-27, 29 (bottom), 31 (top), 34 (top), 35 (top left), 36 (left), 37 (bottom). **John Robinson:** pages 12-13. **Valley Rockery:** page 65. **Martha Rosman:** pages 25 (bottom right), 49. **Julius Shulman:** page 33 (right). **Douglas M. Simmonds:** page 21 (bottom). **Blair Stapp:** page 39 (right). **Tennessee Valley Authority:** page 14 (bottom). **Darrow Watt:** pages 16 (top left), 23 (right), 25 (bottom left), 43, 67. **R. Wenkam:** pages 17 (top), 22-23, 27 (right), 28 (left), bottom right), 41, 61 (left). **Robert Young Studios:** pages 35 (top right), 53.